WATER EXERCISE

MELISSA LAYNE

HUMAN KINETICS

Cataloging-in-Publication Data

Layne, Melissa.
  Water exercise / Melissa Layne.
     pages cm
  Includes bibliographical references and index.
  1. Aquatic exercises. 2. Aerobic exercises. I. Title.
  RA781.17.L39 2015
  613.7'16--dc23

                          2015010724

ISBN: 978-1-4504-9814-2 (print)

The web addresses cited in this text were current as of January 2015, unless otherwise noted.

Acquisitions Editor: Michelle Maloney; **Developmental Editor:** Kevin Matz; **Managing Editor:** Nicole O'Dell; **Copyeditor:** Tom Tiller; **Graphic Designer:** Denise Lowry; **Cover Designer:** Keith Blomberg; **Photographer (interior):** David Haas; photos © Human Kinetics; **Photo Production Manager:** Jason Allen; **Visual Production Assistant:** Joyce Brumfield; **Printer:** Versa Press

We thank the Hugh Mills Physical Education Complex at University of North Georgia, Gainesville, for assistance in providing the location for the photo shoot for this book.

Human Kinetics books are available at special discounts for bulk purchase. Special editions or book excerpts can also be created to specification. For details, contact the Special Sales Manager at Human Kinetics.

Printed in the United States of America   10   9   8   7   6   5   4   3   2   1

The paper in this book is certified under a sustainable forestry program.

Human Kinetics
Website: www.HumanKinetics.com

United States: Human Kinetics, P.O. Box 5076, Champaign, IL 61825-5076
800-747-4457
e-mail: humank@hkusa.com

Canada: Human Kinetics, 475 Devonshire Road Unit 100, Windsor, ON N8Y 2L5
800-465-7301 (in Canada only)
e-mail: info@hkcanada.com

Europe: Human Kinetics, 107 Bradford Road, Stanningley, Leeds LS28 6AT, United Kingdom
+44 (0) 113 255 5665
e-mail: hk@hkeurope.com

Australia: Human Kinetics, 57A Price Avenue, Lower Mitcham, South Australia 5062
08 8372 0999
e-mail: info@hkaustralia.com

New Zealand: Human Kinetics, P.O. Box 80, Torrens Park, South Australia 5062
0800 222 062
e-mail: info@hknewzealand.com

E6332

WATER
EXERCISE

Contents

PREFACE

Water exercise has been popular since 1978, and it is becoming more popular as an effective and gentle form of exercise. It is a great way to stay active regardless of your age and body shape. If you are just starting an activity or fitness program, water is an environment that keeps the joints virtually free of impact, supports you in an upright position (thereby decreasing the potential for falls), and cools the internal body temperature so that overheating is not an issue. If you need a more intense workout, water can provide resistance to your movement that is not found on land and can also be manipulated to challenge you even if you are extremely conditioned. If you have medical concerns, water is a gentle and forgiving environment because it allows you to take the weight off an injured body part while still engaging and strengthening the muscles surrounding that joint. It also permits you to take a break when needed and to set your own pace and intensity, allowing for a truly appropriate training stimulus based on your specific needs. For these and many other reasons, water exercise truly is for everyone.

Water Exercise is for all who are interested in starting water exercise, including those seeking rehabilitation from surgery or injury. The book is divided into four parts. We start with the unique benefits of an aquatic environment and why it is such a valuable part of an activity program. Also in part I are the steps to preparing for a water exercise program, including what equipment, if any, you may need and where you can find it. We also address some specific safety concerns that you need to be aware of in the pool environment.

Once you are ready to get wet, part II will guide you through basic exercises. Using step-by-step written instructions, we give you the basic information for completing the moves. The moves are divided into groups based on the specific body part the activity targets. We start with movements for beginners and then progress into intermediate and advanced options. If you are looking for a workout free of impact, we also have a chapter on deep-water exercise. Deep-water exercise is also a great way to target your heart with a cardiorespiratory workout. All of the exercises are accompanied by photos to help you with the movements. We also offer tips for making the movement easier and progressing the movement to the next level of intensity.

The pool is an excellent place for you if you need specific adaptations after surgery or injury. In part III we address rehabilitation issues from specific injuries and common surgeries. Similar to the previous chapters in the book, the chapters in part III are arranged by the major joints involved, including the and the spine. This makes it easy to find what you are looking for and start building a healthier body. The rehabilitation programs include recent research and a table of previously explained exercises for common joint replacements; overuse injuries such as tendinitis and sprains; and common traumatic injuries such as sprains, tears, and fractures.

Part IV of *Water Exercise* provides a complete fitness workout using the exercises in the previous chapters, so it's like having a fitness trainer take you through a workout at your own convenience. This is directed toward those looking for an all-inclusive cross-training regimen of cardiorespiratory training, muscular endurance, and flexibility. The final chapter is devoted to special populations, including pregnant women, and those with fibromyalgia and Parkinson's disease.

From the sedentary to the fit, aquatic exercise is adaptable to all. It is especially helpful for those with limitations in moving on land. Listen to what your body is telling you as you move through these exercises, and you will find your body responding in a positive way for a more positive life.

PART I

GETTING STARTED

As you begin your adventure in water exercise, chapter 1 introduces you to the unique properties of water that make the pool such a safe and effective place to exercise. The cooling and buoyant properties keep you comfortable while adding physiological benefits such as increased cardiorespiratory endurance and a balanced workout for any postural problems. General guidelines for frequency, duration, and intensity are included in chapter 1.

Chapter 2 focuses on safety in the pool both for swimmers and nonswimmers. Exercise in the water is safe as long as you follow basic safety guidelines and procedures. Some equipment may make you feel more comfortable in the deeper areas of the pool, and other equipment will actually challenge your comfort level. We address many types of the equipment available, but it is important to remember that all you really need is your body and a pool.

CHAPTER I

BASICS OF WATER EXERCISE

Water exercise offers a great way to get in shape, stay in shape, or rehabilitate an injured part of the body. The pool is a forgiving environment because the water cushions and supports your body while reducing the impact on your bones and joints. Another reason that aquatic activity remains popular is that it offers a fabulous way to exercise regardless of what kind of shape you are in. You can easily individualize each workout in terms of speed, intensity, and amount of rest.

Water exercise offers a range of therapeutic and health care benefits for everyone. It also improves all of the fitness components addressed by land exercise. Over time, aquatic exercise can improve your overall health, increase your longevity, and make the activities of your daily life easier while also protecting your body from unnecessary physical stress.

PROPERTIES OF WATER

The properties of water that make aquatic exercise safe and effective are buoyancy, hydrostatic pressure, and viscosity. These properties enable a balanced, low-impact workout that is safe both for people who want to increase their overall fitness and for those seeking rehabilitation after surgery or injury. In addition, the dynamics of thermoregulation in the pool help keep the body cool, thus making aquatic activity a safer and more comfortable mode of exercise, especially for people with certain health conditions, such as pregnancy and fibromyalgia.

Buoyancy

The greatest advantage provided by working in the pool is buoyancy, which is the upward pressure exerted by fluid—in other words, the opposite of gravity's downward pull. You can easily observe the effect of buoyancy by holding an object, such as a playground ball, at the bottom of the pool, then releasing it and watching it pop up to the water's surface. Buoyancy accounts for the feeling of relative weightlessness that we experience in water. It also decreases the compressive forces experienced by the joints, including those in the spine. As a result, aquatic exercise is a low-impact activity.

The amount of benefit provided by buoyancy for exercise depends on the depth of the water. If you stand in water that reaches your navel or belly button (see figure 1.1a), you reduce the impact on your joints by 50 percent. However, though this reduction is sizable, it may not be enough to enable the majority of people to exercise comfortably. If, instead, you position yourself in water that reaches mid-chest or nipple level (see figure 1.1b), you reduce the impact by 75 percent. This depth is comfortable for most people, even those who do not possess strong swimming skills.

People who are fit and looking to cross-train in the water may want to do so at a depth where the water reaches the collar bone (see figure 1.1c). This depth reduces impact by 90 percent and makes it more difficult to maintain one's balance. When balance is challenged, the core muscles in the torso will be forced to contract so the abdominal muscles are more greatly challenged. For the same reason, however, it is often uncomfortable for people who are not strong swimmers. Moving into the deep end to perform suspended exercises removes all impact from the joints but most often requires a flotation device, such as a suspension belt or noodle. It also requires a high level of self-confidence

Figure 1.1 The depth of the water determines the amount of impact placed on the body. The chest level is the most common depth for successful water exercise.

in the water because the body often tilts away from the upright position. For example, your feet may float, which may leave you horizontal in the water, either faceup or facedown.

With all of these factors in mind, chest level is the most common depth for successful water exercise.

Buoyancy also aids flexibility—the range of motion around a joint—which is a primary component of rehabilitation after injury or surgery. Because water provides buoyancy and reduces gravitational force, it allows the exerciser to move his or her limbs more freely, and possibly without pain, toward the surface of the water. Because buoyancy is greatest in deep water, rehabilitation often begins in water deep enough to eliminate gravitational pull on the injured body part and allow the joint to float freely to the water's surface.

Hydrostatic Pressure

Hydrostatic pressure can be defined as the pressure exerted or transmitted by a fluid to an object. The hydrostatic pressure of water molecules creates equal pressure on all parts of the body, and this pressure increases with the depth of the water. This characteristic of water provides great benefits for persons with swelling due to injury, edema from pregnancy, or cardiac concerns. Specifically, any edema or swelling of a joint is decreased when the joint is submerged in water because the fluid in the joint is forced into the capillaries by the hydrostatic pressure of the water against the body, thus returning to the bloodstream. From there, it eventually passes through the kidneys for elimination from the body. This benefit is more noticeable in the lower limbs because they are positioned at a greater depth where the pressure is greater. As a result, for example, pregnant women see a noticeable decrease in ankle swelling.

The hydrostatic pressure of water also facilitates the efficiency of the cardiovascular system, thus making the pool a popular environment for persons recovering from a cardiac incident. Because hydrostatic pressure causes constriction of blood vessels, the heart is pumping blood through a smaller area; as a result, it does not have to pump as often, and the heart rate decreases. Therefore, if you monitor your heart rate while exercising in the water, you may find fewer heartbeats even if you feel you are working more intensely.

Viscosity

Water molecules also provide resistance in every direction, which means that you work opposing muscle groups at the same time. This resistance is caused by the fact that water molecules are cohesive; that is, they stick to each other, and this quality is often referred to as "drag." To push through these sticky molecules, your body must exert muscular force that is 12 to 15 times greater than the force needed when moving through air.

Therefore, water's viscosity helps you develop muscular fitness. It also provides a stabilizing effect that helps the body remain upright, which makes the water a safe place to exercise for people with conditions that affect balance, such as multiple sclerosis and hip replacement. For example, if you lose your balance in the pool, there is no danger of falling and breaking a bone because the water supports you.

Water molecules also possess a property called adhesion, which causes them to stick to other things in the pool, such as pool noodles, clothing, webbed gloves, and even skin. As a result, you can make your workout either more or less intense by adjusting factors such as how you dress, how you hold your hands in the pool, and the position in which you hold a pool noodle (either horizontal or vertical (see figure 1.2). If such factors allow water molecules to adhere to more surface area, your workout is harder. For example, more clothing or baggy clothing creates more surface area, thus making it harder for you to move. A tight-fitting swimsuit, however, provides less surface area to which molecules can stick, thus making your workout easier.

The same thing applies to how you move your hand. Positioning your hand so that it slices through the water with a point leading the way makes your movement easier—similar to the way in which a boat's pointed nose cuts through the

Figure 1.2 Holding a noodle horizontal makes the exercise more difficult (a) than holding it vertical (b).

water. In contrast, holding your hand open in a flat palm that meets the water's surface provides more surface area to which water molecules can stick, thus making it harder for you to move—similar to a pontoon boat with a squared front end.

If your focus is rehabilitation, water's viscosity helps you develop strength and endurance in the injured joint and surrounding muscles. Specifically, the viscosity provides you with balanced resistance regardless of the direction in which you move a limb. Imagine, for instance, that you are rehabbing after an injury to your back. You move your arms forward, as if hugging a tree, then move your arms behind your back as if stretching after getting out of bed. As you perform these movements, the water provides resistance both while you move your arms forward and while you move them backward. This balanced resistance prevents one muscle from getting stronger than the other—a condition that can result in uneven pulling on a tendon, which in turn can cause inflammation or tendinitis.

Thermoregulation

Thermoregulation is a property of the body that increases your comfort level during exercise in the water. In the case of water exercise, the dynamics of thermoregulation mean simply that, as long as you exercise in water that is cooler than you are, you can regulate your body temperature by transferring body heat directly to the water rather than by sweating. Thermoregulation becomes more important as we age due to changes in sweat glands that occur with age; older people experience a progressive decline in the ability to perspire. The typical temperature range of water in a climate-controlled pool is 78 to 82 degrees Fahrenheit (about 25 to 28 degrees Celsius), which allows the body to regulate itself by passing heat to the water molecules.

Although thermoregulation is a property of the human body, it plays a role in the property of water called the specific heat capacity. There are very few other substances that have a higher specific heat capacity than water. This simply means, for our information, that the water requires a large amount of heat to raise the temperature and once the temperature is raised, it takes a good bit of time to cool. The breaking of hydrogen bonds in the H20 molecules requires a large amount of energy, so the energy that is transferred to the water is held in the molecules. You can observe the effects of thermoregulation and the specific heat capacity of water by comparing a pool full of people to a pool only containing water. The crowded pool is warmer because the people pass body heat to the cooler surrounding water but it will not get to the temperature that breaks the hydrogen bonds and turns water into steam because of the high specific heat capacity. This property makes water exercise a comfortable mode of activity for everyone.

There are variables to consider in certain situations. For example, if you are focused on decreasing spasticity—as may be the case with Parkinson's disease, multiple sclerosis, cerebral palsy, or stroke—you might want to exercise in water that is warmer than 85 degrees Fahrenheit (about 29 degrees Celsius). Using warmer water decreases the body's ability to thermoregulate, which is helpful in this case because warming the muscles decreases spasticity.

GENERAL BENEFITS OF WATER EXERCISE

In addition to providing the specific exercise benefits we have just discussed, water also provides the same general benefits offered by land exercise. These benefits can help you increase your life span, improve the quality of your life, and handle daily life activities more comfortably and perhaps more easily. Let's look more closely at four of these benefits: better cardiac health, better body composition, reduced stress, and improved musculoskeletal fitness.

Improved Cardiac Health

Water exercise improves all facets of heart health, which is also known as cardiovascular or cardiorespiratory fitness. Cardiovascular fitness involves the ability of the heart, lungs, and blood vessels to carry oxygen to working muscles. Many people consider this ability to be centrally important for any fitness program because heart disease remains the number one killer of people throughout the world. Cardiovascular fitness is developed with activities that use large muscle groups in continuous movement, including water exercise.

One of the best and easiest ways to assess your cardiovascular health on a regular basis is to monitor your resting heart rate. Choose a day when you can wake up naturally—that is, *not* due to anything like an alarm, the sound of garbage cans being slammed outside your home, or a cat jumping on your head. When you first wake up, while you are still horizontal in bed, find your pulse by placing your hand over your heart and counting the "lub" of the "lub-dub" sound. Count for one full minute. The result is your resting heart rate. As you progress through your workouts, you should see a drop in your resting heart rate. This change means that your heart is becoming more efficient. The better shape you are in, the lower your resting heart rate.

Your resting heart rate is one of the most effective indicators of your heart's health. As your heart gets bigger and stronger, it can pump more blood per stroke. As a result, it doesn't have to pump as often, which means that it beats fewer times per minute at rest. Therefore, your heart rate gives you an easy indicator for self-monitoring your heart health.

If you take your heart rate in the morning by counting your pulse for one minute before you get out of bed, you can see the changes that occur as your exercise program progresses. As you strengthen your heart through exercise, you will see that your resting heart rate decreases because your heart doesn't have to work as hard. Simply put, as your heart becomes stronger, it will be able to fulfill its function with less stress.

Regular exercise also decreases your blood pressure partly because it strengthens your heart and also because it reduces the plaque lining in your veins and arteries. As you make exercise a regular part of your life, your liver makes more of the healthy (HDL) cholesterol, which acts as a scavenger to remove the unhealthy (LDL) cholesterol from the walls of your arteries. This process gives your blood more room to pass freely through your vessels, which decreases your blood pressure.

Another way in which resistance exercise reduces your blood pressure is by prompting your body to create more capillaries. As you push your arms and legs through the water, you slowly increase the size of your muscle fibers. As these fibers increase in size, your body creates more capillaries to carry blood to your muscles. The more capillaries you have, the more room there is for your blood to flow, thus decreasing your blood pressure. One easy way to understand this process is to think of rush hour traffic. If you have fewer streets (capillaries) and lots of cars (blood cells), the pressure is high. When you build more streets or capillaries, you have more room for the cars or blood cells, and the pressure decreases.

In addition, since your heart works closely with your lungs, exercise improves your lung capacity and breathing efficiency. Through this improvement in your breathing processes, exercise also aids in the circulation of oxygen and nutrients throughout your body, thereby helping it operate more efficiently.

Improved Body Composition

Any type of exercise that causes your body to burn more calories for energy increases your chance of changing your body composition, which is determined by the proportions of lean and non-lean tissue in your body mass. Lean tissue components are tendons, ligaments, and muscle, whereas non-lean tissue is adipose or fat tissue. You burn more fat cells as a form of energy when you increase your caloric expenditure by exercising in the pool.

In order to decrease the fat mass in your body, you must create a calorie deficit; that is, you must burn more calories than you take in. As your fat-to-lean tissue ratio drops, your percentage of lean tissue (fat-free mass) increases. You can also directly increase your fat-free mass or lean tissue by increasing your resistance work. As we have seen, the pool facilitates this work by providing built-in resistance due to the viscosity of the water that you must push through every time you move. As a result, over time, your clothes may begin to fit better, and you may start to see small changes when you stand on the scale.

Of course, body composition can also be affected positively by initiating and maintaining healthy eating patterns. If you eat a well-balanced diet, you should see a shift in your body composition to a higher percentage of lean mass and a lower percentage of fat mass. The benefits of this change include an increase in the ability of most organs to function effectively while experiencing less stress, thereby possibly increasing your life span and your quality of life.

Reduced Stress

Psychological stress can damage our DNA and increase our risk of age-related disease. In contrast, exercise protects DNA and slows down the aging process. In fact, though it may sound odd, exercise itself constitutes a certain type of stress—called hormesis—that is good for the body. Specifically, moderate-intensity exercise increases certain brain-derived factors that maintain brain health; this type of stress may even reverse the effects of chronic negative stress on the brain.

Other psychological benefits of exercise include improved self-image, more efficient brain function, and an increase in one's sense of well-being. Research also shows that exercise helps slow memory loss and may even improve short-term memory. All of these benefits can improve our quality of life and help us become happier people.

Improved Musculoskeletal Fitness

Exercise also benefits our bones and muscles in many ways, and these benefits are particularly important in societies where a sedentary lifestyle is the norm. Musculoskeletal fitness includes muscular endurance and muscular strength. Muscular endurance consists of a muscle's ability to contract repeatedly against a force—for our purposes here, the resistance exerted by water. Muscular strength, on the other hand, consists of a muscle's ability to contract one time as forcefully as possible. The majority of your work in the water targets endurance, but some people starting a rehabilitation program also see an increase in strength because the injured limb, joint, or muscle has decreased in size, mobility, or strength.

The benefits of working the musculoskeletal system include improved posture, reduced blood pressure, and decreased risk of injury in daily life. On a practical level, you will find it easier to perform the activities of daily living. For example, you may notice that it is easier than it used to be to get up from the floor or sit down in a chair because your leg muscles are stronger. Similarly, you may see strength gains that make activities easier. For example, you may be able to move furniture on your own or find that your gait or walking pattern has become more stable because the muscles surrounding your hip joints are stronger.

Muscular exercise also makes your bones stronger and increases their density, thus decreasing your risk of osteoporosis. This condition, characterized by loss of bone mass, is seen more often in females than in males and tends to affect the hips, spine, and wrists. Muscular endurance also helps protect your bones by increasing your body's efficiency of skeletal support, which is the ability to hold your body erect so that you are less likely to lose your balance and fall. In addition, exercise increases the flow of synovial fluid (a lubricant) around the joints and slows the degeneration of joints.

One quality that is closely related to muscular fitness is flexibility, which is the range of motion around a joint. Flexibility is most often associated with stretching, but it can also be aided simply by moving your muscles through a full range of motion, even if you don't hold the stretch. This work is facilitated in the water by the buoyancy factor. To see how, stand in chest-deep water and relax your arms by your side. If you are truly relaxed and not thinking about it, your arms rise to the surface of the water. The same thing happens if you stand in chest-deep water and begin to lift one leg in front of you slightly off the bottom of the pool. Once you have initiated the movement, the leg will continue to lift due to buoyancy. As these examples illustrate, the pool is a great place to increase a joint's range of motion after injury or surgery because no one has to exert pressure or undue force on the joint. Generally, the benefits of a flexible body are similar to the benefits of a strong body. They also include decreased chronic back pain and a reduced chance of strains and sprains.

The muscular improvements provided by exercise also reduce your risk of injury by strengthening your tendons and ligaments, thus helping you keep your balance. If you maintain a good exercise program for an extended period of time, you will experience increases in your muscular strength, muscular endurance, and flexibility. Most important, consistent exercise helps you maintain muscle mass, which slows the typical age-related decline in metabolism. Metabolism is the combination of physical and chemical processes occurring within the body's cells that are necessary for the maintenance of life. We want to elevate our rate of metabolism as much as possible. Maintaining muscle mass or adding muscle mass increases the amount of energy that our body needs to continue life processes.

EXERCISE GUIDELINES AND PROGRESSIVE OVERLOAD

The first step in undertaking any exercise or rehabilitation program is to get clearance from your doctor. If you are beginning a program for rehabilitation, get approval for water exercise from a medical specialist who possesses current knowledge of your situation. Your specialist may set specific guidelines for how often or how long you should perform aquatic activity. If you are beginning a fitness regimen and are a healthy adult, obtain approval from your general practitioner for your water exercise program.

Exercise guidelines for injury-free adults are provided by the American College of Sports Medicine. These guidelines include protocols for key aspects of exercise: frequency, intensity, and duration. Frequency is how often you perform an activity. The general recommendation is to exercise three to five times per week or to do easier activities (such as gardening or taking the stairs instead of the elevator) on most or all days of the week.

Intensity is determined by how hard you work, and it is inversely proportional to how long you work out. For example, if you are just beginning, the guidelines suggest starting at a lower intensity for 15 to 20 minutes. As your body adjusts to the workload, you can either increase your intensity (while maintaining the same duration) or increase your duration (while sticking with the lower intensity). This process is called progressive overload, and it simply means that you make your workout either a bit more intense or a bit longer each week.

Another simple way to progressively overload your program is to increase the frequency of your workouts. As you begin your program, always take a day off between exercise sessions. This approach gives your muscles—including your heart—a chance to rest and recover. Thanks to the day off, your rested muscles will be ready to perform again 48 hours after your last workout. Over time, your muscles adapt to the exercises and perform more efficiently. As a result, as you progress through the program, you may not need as long to recover. Therefore, you may progress to daily workouts. One good tip to remember is to alternate the intensity of your workouts on consecutive days. For example, if you do a shorter but more intense workout on Monday, do a longer but less intense workout on Tuesday.

As you begin your water exercise program, be sure to progress safely and slowly. This deliberate approach both minimizes the risk of injury and keeps you psychologically fresh. If you progress gradually, you will begin to look forward to the many benefits of exercise, including the release of endorphins—the chemical messengers that tell your brain how great you feel after a workout.

As you work through the exercises in this book, remember that drag increases as movement increases. As a result, when you travel through the water, drag makes your workout more intense. Therefore, when you first attempt an exercise, do it in place, without traveling. For example, consider the staples of water exercise: walking, jogging, and running. These activities are easier to perform when remaining in place than when moving across the pool. Progressing from doing any exercise in place to doing that same exercise moving across the pool will make it more intense due to the fact that drag increases as movement increases. This is a simple example of progressive overload.

Another way to slowly progress an exercise is to increase the length of what we might refer to as a bodily lever. For our purposes here, the main levers of your body are your arms and legs. When you use a short lever, the load is easier to lift. When you use a long lever, the load is more difficult to lift. Think of it in terms of moving a large rock with a plank. You can move the rock more readily with a shorter lever (plank) under the rock than with a longer lever. It works the same way in the water. For example, it is easier on your shoulder joint to perform a jumping jack with your elbows bent at a ninety-degree angle than with a straight elbow.

Imagine yourself in the water doing knee lifts. A knee lift involves a ninety-degree bend of the knee joint. It is less difficult for your hip joint to lift the bone in your thigh (see figure 1.3a) than to lift a longer lever composed of the bones in both your upper leg and your lower leg (see figure 1.3b). Straight arms and straight legs also create more drag than bent limbs. Keep these helpful hints in mind as you choose the exercises for your daily workout so that you can make it less intense or more intense as needed on any given day.

You can also increase the intensity of your workout by using certain types of equipment. For example, you can use various pieces of equipment (such as webbed gloves) to increase the surface area of your body and thereby increase drag. Other pieces of equipment (such as pool noodles) are buoyant and therefore require you to use more muscular strength to push beneath the

Figure 1.3   Short levers are easier to lift (a). Long levers are harder to lift (b).

water. Regardless of how you choose to handle progressive overload in your workout, it is crucial that you listen to your body and work at your own pace as your body adapts to the increased workload.

You have now gained an understanding of how the human body moves in the water and how to begin your physical workout. The next chapter addresses equipment options and what to look for to ensure a safe environment for water exercise.

CHAPTER 2

PREPARING TO GET WET

Think about the last time you went to the airport, whether to board a flight or offer a ride to someone. Before you arrived, you had to have a great deal of information on hand to make the trip as enjoyable, stress free, and successful as possible. For instance, you had to know which terminal to go to, what time to be there, where to park, and whom to see—all before even approaching the plane. Unfortunately, most people do more research for a plane trip than they do before embarking on a fitness program. But fear not! This chapter gives you all the information you need in order to begin your fitness journey.

HOW TO FIND A POOL

The most convenient place to do water exercise would be a pool in the privacy of your own home. However, since most of us do not have that convenience, we must look elsewhere—but where? Research shows that people continue a workout program with greater regularity if the facility is close to either home or work and fits conveniently into their daily life. With this reality in mind, set your sights close to home and research the obvious choices, such as neighborhood pools, YMCAs, aquatic centers, recreation centers, and health club facilities.

If you don't find such a facility that fits your preferences, think outside of the box. For example, many hotels offer access to their guest pool at a daily or monthly rate. In addition, these pools often offer the advantage of being enclosed or climate controlled, thus allowing you to exercise comfortably throughout the year.

Alternatively, do you have a friend or neighbor who owns a pool? Research also shows that people continue a workout program more reliably when they have a workout partner to whom they are accountable. It is not quite as easy to excuse yourself when someone else has committed to the same day and time.

If you would like some initial guidance about your water workout, consider using a pool with a water fitness program. Some facilities offer a wide variety of classes, perhaps including various levels of intensity. If you choose to participate in a water fitness program with an instructor, arrive early to class on the first day and introduce yourself. Let the instructor know your current level of fitness, discuss any medical concerns, and ask any general questions you may have about the class.

Before you commit to such a program, make sure that the instructor is certified by a water-fitness authority (not merely a land-fitness certifying body). The instructor should also be certified in CPR. These certifications must be renewed every one or two years to keep the instructor up to date on the newest research about water fitness and rehabilitation.

SAFETY IN THE POOL ENVIRONMENT

When you explore your options, and before you commit to a pool membership, look for key safety indicators—not only in the pool itself but also in the general pool environment. The majority of injuries sustained in water fitness programs happen, not in the water, but on the pool deck. Look for nonslip traction aids both on the deck and on the surfaces used to enter the pool; for example, steps and stairs should feature a nonslip surface and a stable handrail. If you use a walker or cane, look for a pool with a chair that can be accessed at the side of the pool and then lowered mechanically into the water.

If you are not a strong swimmer, or are just not comfortable in the water, consider looking for a facility that provides an on-duty lifeguard during the hours when you plan to exercise. At the same time, one great thing about vertical exercise in the water is that it does not require you to be a strong swimmer. You just need to be comfortable lifting one foot off the floor of the pool. For exercises that involve lifting both feet off the bottom, you can stay close to the side of the pool; that way, if you feel uncomfortable at any time, you can just reach out and grab the wall. You might also want to look for a pool that offers various depths so that you can work in both the shallow and deep ends in order to change your impact options and increase the variety of exercises available.

Survey the pool surroundings and note whether a life-saving device is available to throw into the pool if someone gets into trouble. Also assess general pool maintenance. For instance, skimmers should all have covers for safety reasons. A skimmer is simply a basket that collects floating debris. However, there is a safety issue if there is not a cover as you could easily trip and fall by accidently stepping into the basket. Lights should all be in working order, electrical outlets should all be grounded, a working telephone should be located close by, and of course the pool itself should be clean and free of debris.

You should also bring a water bottle as a safety precaution to avoid dehydration. Many people think that dehydration is impossible in a pool environment, but it does occur in warm, humid environments, both indoors and outdoors. In fact, as discussed in chapter 1, you transfer body heat into the water by means of thermoregulation. To prevent dehydration, take a break to drink water whenever you feel that you want or need a sip of fluid. Drink more if you exercise in a pool environment with a higher temperature, such as an outdoor pool in the summer. For workouts lasting 60 minutes or fewer, water is sufficient—the average person does not require additional electrolytes or sugar solutions for workouts of this duration.

Temperature Concerns

As mentioned in chapter 1, climate-controlled fitness pools generally have a water temperature in the low 80s Fahrenheit (the upper 20s Celsius). Pools geared specifically for lap swimmers may be slightly cooler (in the high 70s Fahrenheit or mid 20s Celsius). If you are looking for a rehabilitation pool, you will see warmer temperatures (in the low 90s Fahrenheit or low 30s Celsius). Any of these pools would enable a good workout for the general population.

However, if you seek rehabilitation—or if you have arthritis, cerebral palsy, multiple sclerosis, or another condition for which you need to decrease the spasticity of muscles—a warmer therapy pool will be more comfortable for you. On the other hand, if you find a convenient pool that generally suits your needs but is on the cool end of the spectrum, you may be able to make it work. For example, you can lengthen your warm-up, use clothing that covers more of your body, or keep your body moving at all times.

Even when you stretch at the conclusion of your workout, you can stay warm by stretching one body part while keeping other parts moving. For example, let's assume that you want to stretch your calf by planting a leg on the pool bottom and straightening that back knee. While you do so, you can keep your arms moving by pretending to hug an imaginary tree in front of you, then pushing through your core to move your arms behind you and open up your chest.

Water Quality

Before committing to a pool membership, check not only the water's temperature but also its quality. The National Swimming Pool Foundation certifies pool and spa operators so that the chemicals are controlled by someone with a certain level of training and knowledge. The pool should be cleaned with chemicals in order to prevent the transmission of communicable diseases.

However, chlorine, bromide, and other chloramines used for pool cleaning may irritate your skin, dry your hair, or cause your swimsuit to fade. If your body is irritated by any of these chemicals, you usually notice it first in the eyes. If needed, feel free to wear goggles to protect your eyes. Also consider wearing a swim cap to cover your hair, even if you will not be submerging your head in the water. Wearing a swim cap will not only keep your hair from getting wet from splashing but will also help keep the hair out of the pool and debris out of the skimmer.

If you choose a pool with a high chemical content, follow the rules you may have learned as a child. Always shower before and after your workout and include a good soaking of your hair and swimsuit. Most people believe that showering before they swim is done to cleanse the body of dirt. This is partially true, but you are also coating your hair and suit with a layer of water molecules that do not contain chlorine or another chemical. Remember the principle of adhesion discussed in chapter 1? Because of adhesion, water molecules from your before-swim shower stick to your suit and your hair strands, thus inhibiting the chemical-containing water molecules in the pool from discoloring your hair or fading your swimsuit.

Clothing

Your clothing for water exercise should be comfortable and fit close to your body. Most participants are comfortable in a one-piece swimsuit that provides adequate support and fits snugly. Clothing that is too loose may slip off as you move through the water; thus, a one-piece swimsuit is the obvious choice.

Shoes are optional, and the decision about whether to wear them often depends on the surface at the bottom of the pool, specifically, how slippery it is. Shoes definitely decrease the risk of slipping on the pool bottom; they also reduce the risk of falling, both on the deck and while getting into the pool. On the other hand, water shoes increase the surface area of your feet, which, as discussed in chapter 1, increases the resistance you will encounter in the water. They may also feel awkward to some people.

There are a couple of additional considerations regarding shoes. If the bottom of the pool is rough, water shoes decrease the risk of blisters and even cuts from sharp imperfections in the concrete. However, if you are working out in the deep end of the pool, shoes may be unnecessary because you will not be touching the pool bottom.

Figure 2.1 Strong (a) versus weak (b) posture.

Posture

During movement, your skeletal system—bones, muscles, tendons, and ligaments—should not be stressed by postural imperfections. Indeed, using good form in your exercise reduces your risk of injury and joint problems; therefore, proper posture is a necessity. You can improve your posture through training if you focus on standing, sitting, and reclining in positions that place the least possible strain on your body's support structures.

When standing in an upright position, you should have a straight-line alignment from your ears through your shoulders, your hips, your knees, and finally your ankles. In addition, the front of your bottom rib should line up with your pelvis, and your spine should run directly down the center of your back. When you move from a standing position to a seated one, your spine should remain centered and straight.

One of the unique benefits of water exercise lies in the balanced resistance provided by the water (see chapter 1 for more detail). This balance means that we work opposing muscles equally on both the front and back of the body, including the postural muscles (see figure 2.1). Because this benefit is missing from land exercise, people who exercise out of the water tend to overwork the muscles on the front of the body, thus leaving the muscles on the back side underused. Over time, this imbalance increases a person's risk of injury.

WATER-SPECIFIC EQUIPMENT

Water exercise requires little or no equipment. You need a pool or some other body of water, of course, but other equipment is optional and is certainly not necessary for getting started. In the United States, equipment can range in price from $1 (for a pool noodle) to $50 (for a set of buoys or hand paddles). Most equipment arrives from the manufacturer with instructions for proper use, and you should follow those instructions. If an instructional video is included, watch it before you integrate the equipment into your program.

Equipment made specifically for water exercise falls into two basic categories: buoyant equipment and surface-area equipment. Neither type is mandatory for an effective workout; indeed, you can get a tremendous workout in the water by using your body as your only equipment. If you do choose to add equipment, first master the basic exercise without the equipment, then slowly add props that fit the size of your body. For example, if a petite woman tries to push a noodle taller than she is through the water, she may end up floating on the noodle instead of controlling it with her muscles. As discussed in chapter 1, however, if you use pool equipment properly, it can help you gradually increase the intensity of your workout to achieve the desired progressive overload.

Buoyant Equipment

Buoyant equipment includes any pool equipment that floats (see figure 2.2). It serves two purposes: (1) to help keep you afloat—though it is *not* meant to be a life-saving device—and (2) to provide additional resistance. For example, you might sit on a noodle, similar to sitting on a swing, and extend your leg at the knee joint to strengthen your upper thigh muscles. Alternatively, you might push the noodle down through the water to help strengthen the muscles in your arms. You can even use a simple beach ball to work your triceps on the back of your upper arms. Hold the ball with both hands, keeping your elbows locked in tightly to your rib cage, and push the ball under the water. You can do the same thing with a pool noodle or kickboard.

Whole-body buoyant devices, such as waist belts (see figure 2.3), can be used for rehabilitation, stretching, relaxation, and deep-water workouts. When using such devices, be aware that the type and size of the flotation device can affect the positioning of your body in the water. For example, if a belt with a large back support is used by someone with a large amount of visceral fat around the waist, especially on the back side, the person may lose vertical alignment

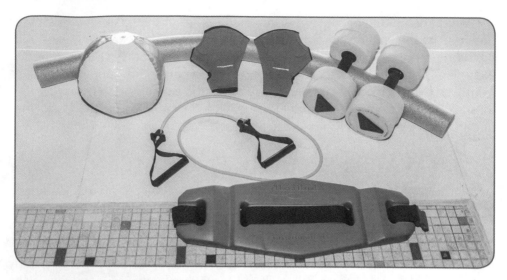

Figure 2.2 A variety of water fitness equipment is available.

by leaning forward. This position makes it challenging for the person simply to hold himself or herself upright. In such cases, it may be beneficial to turn the belt around.

Other buoyant devices, such as ankle cuffs, are worn around the limbs, but they are not used to increase resistance for those limbs. Rather, they are used to create neutral buoyancy, meaning that they help you keep your body upright (vertical) and your head above water. Buoyant devices are used when the exercise is done in a position in the pool where the feet are not touching the bottom of the pool. This is often the case during rehabilitation of a joint if the joint cannot support any weight of the body at that particular time. The buoyant equipment allows the participant to move the injured joint, or any active joint, through a full range of motion without the stress of any impact forces. The extent to which a given person's body floats or sinks depends on overall body composition. More lean muscle mass creates a denser body, which sinks more readily; as a result, a more muscular person may require help from flotation devices in order to keep the head above the water. Indeed, athletes may need to use a buoyant ankle cuff on each ankle, as well as a belt.

When using flotation equipment for an exercise session, sit on the edge of the pool at the shallow end, put the equipment on, and then slide into the water. Avoid jumping into the deep end while wearing the buoyancy equipment; instead, get comfortable with the equipment

Figure 2.3 Waist belt.

in the shallow end before you venture into deep water. Buoyancy devices take some getting used to, and it requires practice to keep your body in a vertical position.

Surface-Area Equipment

Surface-area equipment includes anything that you can put into the pool to increase the surface area to which water molecules can adhere (see chapter 1 for more about adhesion). It might even be the same equipment used for buoyancy. For example, if you do water-walking laps in the pool without any equipment and would like to make your workout slightly more intense, simply hold a noodle horizontal just under the surface of the water and walk with the noodle in front of you. The adherence of water molecules to the noodle makes you push harder as you move forward, thus increasing your workout intensity and therefore the number of calories you burn.

Another popular option involves wearing webbed gloves (see figure 2.4) that increase the surface area to which water molecules can stick as you move your hands through the water. The resulting increase in drag means that the muscles in your arms have to work harder; therefore, wearing webbed gloves is one way to achieve progressive overload. Webbed gloves also give you a wider, more stable surface as you push your hands flat into the water. This surface provides you with an extra buoyant lift and helps you vertically stabilize your upper body.

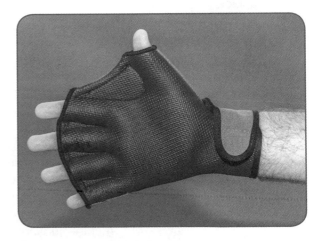

Figure 2.4 Webbed gloves.

Remember to begin exercises with no equipment, then slowly incorporate appropriate equipment into your sessions. In addition, always listen to your body and take the necessary time to specifically locate any discomfort you feel. Muscle discomfort is usually a sign that you are overloading your workout, whereas joint discomfort is your body's way of telling you that something isn't quite right. With all of this in mind, one great thing about gloves is that they are easy to remove if you feel discomfort at any point in your workout.

Water buoys and plastic fitness paddles are often used for progressive overloading during a water fitness workout. Although these pieces of equipment float, none are used to keep the participant from touching the bottom of the pool as the ankle cuffs and buoyant belts are. These pieces of equipment are used to increase the surface area of the limb or limbs that you are working. An example would be sweeping a straight arm across the front of your body from the right to the left side. A straight arm moved underneath the water is difficult.

When you add to the surface area of your arm by adding a paddle or a buoy in your hand, the movement becomes even more difficult because of the added surface area to which the water molecules adhere.

Most manufacturers offer water buoys and fitness paddles in various sizes and shapes. When purchasing such equipment, consider your body strength and size—bigger is not always better. If the equipment is too large for a person's size or ability, the tendency is to compensate by recruiting additional muscle groups in movement patterns that are not anatomically correct or safe. For example, if a fitness paddle is too large for a person's shoulder joint to correctly swing it though the water like a tennis racket, he or she tends to recruit the wrist joint, which can lead to an overuse injury such as tendinitis.

Here is a basic rule for choosing the right size of equipment: You should be able to perform 8 to 12 repetitions before the targeted muscle (or muscle group) begins to fatigue. If at any time your body alignment is compromised—that is, if you cannot maintain the proper posture as discussed earlier—remove the equipment from your workout.

Kickboards are readily available at many pools, and they can be used to increase surface area, or to manipulate as a resistance piece. You can also use a kickboard to stabilize your torso while performing an exercise that works your legs. You have probably seen swimmers who want to improve their swim kick hold a kickboard underneath their torsos or out in front of their bodies as they move through the pool. Indeed, kickboards are so versatile that they can often be used instead of more expensive pieces of equipment. Be aware, however, that if you do not have a good grip on a kickboard while it is underwater, it may slip out of your grasp, pop up forcefully out of the water, and hit you.

Another popular option is exercise tubing (see figure 2.5), which provides a way to increase your strength training or advance your rehabilitation efforts. It does not fall under either water-specific category of equipment—buoyant or surface-area—and in fact it is often used on land because the muscle actions created by rubberized equipment are similar in any environment. This type of equipment usually consists of a band or tubing with handles, and it comes in multiple colors to differentiate the levels of intensity. The color scheme may vary, so you can check with the manufacturer to see which colors indicate light, medium, and heavy resistance. Keep in mind that the chemicals in the pool will degrade the rubber in the tubing. If you choose to use rubber tubing, always inspect it for cracks or tears before your work out. As soon as you see the tubing is damaged, discard it and replace it with a new piece of rubberized equipment.

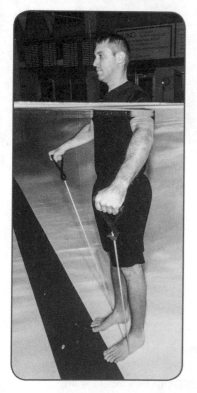

Figure 2.5   Exercise tubing.

If this summary of equipment options seems overwhelming, please remember that you can reap the benefits of water exercise without any additional equipment. Indeed, the mass of your body is a piece of equipment in itself, and you should start your workout without any other equipment. Then, when you get to the point where you feel a need for progressive overload, you can return to this chapter for options.

You can find online sources for equipment and swimsuits in the following list. Also consider visiting a local sporting goods store, where you may find a knowledgeable associate to answer your specific questions. If you do choose to order online, the following resources are good places to begin.

Amazon.com—clothing and equipment

Aquagear.com—clothing and equipment

Aquajogger.com—equipment

Hydrofit.com—equipment

Isokineticsinc.com—equipment

Kiefer.com—clothing and equipment

Power-systems.com—equipment

Sprintaquatics.com—equipment

Swimoutlet.com—clothing and equipment

Thelifeguardstore.com—equipment

Theraquatics.com—equipment

Once again, the only equipment that you truly need is a pool and your body. Everything else is optional and should be used only as you progress safely into your workout regimen.

We turn now to the workout itself. It begins with a warm-up, which is the subject of the next chapter. The photos and discussion provided therein walk you safely through the process of priming your body for the main workout, which is addressed in the following chapters. Let's get wet!

PART II

CHOOSING YOUR EXERCISES

Now that you are familiar with the benefits and unique properties of water exercises, it is time to start planning your workout. In chapter 3 you will find exercises for the warm-up and the flexibility segments. Always remember to include these basic movements so that your body is ready to proceed to the exercises in chapters 4 through 7. The latter chapters are structured according to intensity of the exercises. If you are new to water fitness, start with the exercises in chapter 4 and become proficient with those. As you become more comfortable and the exercises in chapter 4 are no longer challenging, you can start adding some exercises from chapters 5 and 6.

Chapter 7 is devoted entirely to deep-water exercises. Deep water is great place to work out if you wish to avoid impact on the joints or only have access to a deep-water pool. When exercising in deep water, you might need a flotation device, but this is the only portion of part II where equipment might be needed. Remember that you can perform all other exercises with only your limbs as equipment.

CHAPTER 3

WARM-UP AND FLEXIBILITY SEGMENT

Once your health care provider clears you to begin a water fitness program, it's time to get in the pool! As with every workout, you should always warm up before starting an exercise session in earnest. Warming up has been the subject of considerable research over the years; thus the American College of Sports Medicine recommends a warm-up lasting 5 to 10 minutes.

Whether your warm-up is on the low end of this time range or the high end depends on many factors. For example, if you are exercising in a warm environment with warm water, your muscles may already be pliable and ready to go, especially if it is later in the day and you have been active for several hours. However, if you are working out in the morning, or if the weather or water temperature is chilly, you will need a longer warm-up.

During your warm-up, your body experiences certain physiological responses. For one thing, of course, your internal body temperature rises. Your heart rate also increases, as do your blood pressure and breathing rate. In addition, as you move your limbs, blood flow to them increases, and your postural muscles also become stretched as blood flow increases to the connective tissue in your core.

In simple terms, your warm-up prepares your body for more efficient and more effective performance by your muscles. This preparation also decreases your risk of injury.

BEGINNING THE WORKOUT

When you first enter the pool, take time to let your body adjust to the temperature of the water. Do some easy marching in place, some reaches with your arms, and, if you have a healthy back, some slow twists. Once your body acclimates to the water temperature, it's time to perform some bigger movements. You might start by water walking from one end of the pool to the other; use your arms as if you were walking on land—that is, reaching each arm forward along with its opposite leg. Water walking engages the muscles that you will later use for more vigorous or specific moves. It also allows your body temperature to rise slowly so that you do not pull a muscle or otherwise hurt yourself.

The U.S. Centers for Disease Control and Prevention has compiled over one hundred studies showing that a warm-up should consist of movements that mimic the intended workout but on a smaller, slower scale. For instance, a runner might warm up with a brisk walk, and a cyclist might ride the bike at a slow pace. In what may be a surprise to some people, these same studies show that static stretching (stretches that are held) impair performance. Static stretching immediately before exercise often causes muscle damage because the muscle is not warmed by previous activity and an increase in blood flow. The muscle damage incurred during static stretching to a cold muscle will actually decrease strength and power of the muscle. Instead, it is recommended that you perform dynamic stretches, which shorten one muscle at the same time that the opposite muscle lengthens. Because dynamic stretching is done while moving, the blood flow to the muscle is increased, and there is little to no muscle damage as seen in the static stretching of a cold muscle. The movement of the area and the concurrent shortening and lengthening of the muscle fibers all increase blood flow and warm the area, creating a safer, less-damaging stretch.

Muscles are organized in pairs, so any move that contracts one muscle stretches another. For example, you may have seen soccer players walk across the field by kicking up one leg at a time and touching the toes of the lifted leg with the fingers of the hand of the opposite arm. In this example, the quadriceps and the iliopsoas muscle group on the front of the lifted leg shorten as the gluteus maximus and hamstring group of muscles of the back of the lifted leg lengthen. The toe is touched with the fingers of the opposite hand because it stretches the muscles in the upper back as the muscles in the front of the chest shorten. Another example is the biceps curl, in which the triceps muscle on the back of the arm stretches at the same time that the biceps on the front of the arm shortens.

It is quite simple to use dynamic stretching in your warm-up. Just gently start moving your limbs, and the muscles on the opposite side of your body will receive a stretch. When you walk forward placing the right leg in front of the left, the muscles in the front of the right leg contract or shorten and the muscles in the back of the right leg lengthen. As you swing the left leg through to take the next step, the muscles in the front of the left leg contract as the muscles in the back of the left leg lengthen.

Sample Warm-Up

The best way to begin your workout is with water walking, water jogging, or water running. Water walking is just like walking on land. With one foot always in contact with the bottom of the pool, swing the back leg through to be placed on the pool bottom hip-width apart but in front of the other leg. Once that foot is in contact with the pool bottom, swing the back leg through and place the foot on the bottom of the pool surface. Continue moving forward as you place one foot in front of the other, hip width apart. Water jogging will require the same swing through of the back leg as water walking. In water jogging, just as in jogging on land, when the back leg swings through, the opposite foot has lost contact with the surface below it, whether it be the pool bottom in water or the pavement on land. Water running is simply a faster form of water jogging. Because running is a faster pace than jogging, the knees will not have the time to lift as high in water running as in water jogging.

Whenever you increase the pace of an exercise, the moves will decrease in size. In water jogging, knees will lift higher as they pass by the other leg. In water running, feet will stay closer to the bottom of the pool as the leg in back passes by the leg that was in the front. All three of these moves are a great start to a work out in the water, and one is not better than another. Start with the one with which you are most comfortable. Start water jogging or water running in place, pushing off the bottom of the pool to move your body upward instead of forward. If you choose to warm up with water walking, you cannot do that in place because you are placing one foot in front of the other without losing contact with the bottom of the pool surface. Once you are comfortable jogging or running in place, slowly begin to move through the water in all directions for a minimum of three minutes (see figure 3.1). This activity slowly raises your heart rate, blood pressure, and body temperature.

The next group of dynamic stretches can be done in any order. Just remember to keep moving without holding position. These stretches keep your body warm and maintain any other physiological adaptations that occurred during your water walking or running.

To perform the standing side stretch (see figure 3.2), assume a grounded position with

Figure 3.1 Water jogging.

Figure 3.2 Standing side stretch.

Figure 3.3 Chest opener.

Figure 3.4 Back stretch.

both feet on the pool bottom. Face the wall and hold on to it, then bend one knee as you shift your weight to that side. When you feel a stretch in your inner thigh, reverse to the other side. You can bend as far as is comfortable to one side while keeping both feet on the bottom surface of the pool. However, the depth of the water will be an obvious stopping point as you do not want to submerge your head as you bend your knee and lower your body into the water. Remember to shift your weight to that side only until you feel slight tension in your inner thigh. Avoid any pain or discomfort. Aim for a total of 10 repetitions (5 per side).

It is also important to open up the muscles in your chest and upper back. In today's sedentary society, many of us spend the majority of the day in a seated position, which tightens the muscles on the front of the body. Therefore, your warm-up should stretch these muscles dynamically—that is, without holding any given position. You can do so by performing the chest opener (see figure 3.3), which resembles the action of hugging a tree and then opening the body. It doesn't matter whether you open the body first or imitate hugging the tree first as it is a dynamic stretch, and you will do one movement and then the other, and then repeat the first movement followed by the second movement.

Figure 3.3 shows the open position, which stretches the front of your body. Figure 3.4 displays the closed position, which stretches the muscles in your upper back so that your body is balanced and less likely to be injured. As you stretch your upper back, think about rounding it like an angry cat. This pulling apart of your inner back muscles helps you achieve a dynamic stretch.

Now, return to the initial position. Your movements should flow smoothly, without a true stop at the full range of motion. Again, try to perform 10 total repetitions (5 in each direction).

To bring your warm-up to a close, try the knee lift and hamstring curl, which provide terrific dynamic stretches for your lower body. As you bring your knee up (see figure 3.5), you stretch your hamstrings and glutes on the posterior side of your body. You may choose to do this dynamic movement either while bouncing off the bottom of the pool or while always keeping one foot in contact with the pool bottom. For a good dynamic stretch, perform a set of 20 alternating repetitions. Count lifting the right leg as one repetition and lifting the left leg as another repetition.

The hamstring curl stretches the opposing set of leg muscles—that is, your quadriceps. As you pull your heel to your glutes, you stretch the muscles on the front of your thigh. Again, it is your choice as to whether you bounce or keep one foot on the pool bottom at all times. In addition, you may feel more comfortable doing this move if you tip forward a bit as you lift your heel to your hip (see figure 3.6). For a good warm-up and stretch, perform a set of 20 alternating hamstring curls. Again, lifting the right leg counts as one repetition, and lifting the left leg counts as a second repetition.

As you begin to move, you may feel the urge to bounce due to the buoyancy of the water. Any bouncing movement in the water is referred to as rebounding, which is perfectly safe during your warm-up as long as you begin with small rebounding moves and progress gradually to any larger ones. Rebounding moves include a tiny bit of time—a split second—in which both feet are off the bottom of the pool. This action is natural in the water due to the water's

Figure 3.5   Dynamic knee lift.

Figure 3.6   Dynamic hamstring curl.

buoyancy, which gives you that familiar feeling of relative weightlessness. It is called rebounding because you step down onto one or both feet, and as you place your foot onto the bottom of the pool, you slightly bend the knee of that same leg and push off the bottom. It is similar to stepping down onto a trampoline at the same time as you bend your knees and bounce. In the pool, you are not fighting the amount of gravity as on the trampoline, so your body will rebound upward with less effort.

In contrast, movements in which you have one or both feet on the pool bottom at all times are referred to as anchored or grounded actions. One example is water walking without bouncing. Another example involves standing still while you push water forcefully with your hands from the right side of your body to the left side of your body. If you choose to do grounded or anchored work during your warm-up, you should extend the length of your warm-up because these moves are less intense than rebounding ones. As a result, your body takes longer to become pliable, and your heart rate remains a bit lower.

As you progress through your 5- to 10-minute warm-up, it is crucial that you focus on maintaining proper posture. Because your posture is controlled by the muscles in your trunk, or core, it is often referred to as core control. By either name, it provides the foundation for functional movements—the movements of our activities of daily life.

Weak abdominal or core muscles can contribute to poor posture, improper body mechanics, and low-back pain. This is why it is important to focus on bracing your core as you work through your water exercises. Many people think that this involves sucking in the stomach, but it does not. In fact, sucking in your stomach puts your lower back into an abnormal curve that can be painful over time.

Instead, simply brace your core region. Specifically, upon exhaling, tighten your core muscles as if you were going to be punched in the stomach and didn't want it to hurt. As you brace your core, you should feel yourself standing a bit taller. Some women may compare this bracing to the feeling of having a corset tightened around the core. Bracing not only protects your vertebrae but also improves your posture.

Moves to Avoid

Two things to leave out of your warm-up are neutral and suspended moves. These moves require your body to be physically primed because they place greater demand on your heart muscle and require more muscle activation. In fact, they are intense enough that they should be included only in the workout that follows the warm-up.

Neutral moves are performed with the shoulders dropped to the level of the water. The knees are bent, and the feet simply slide across the bottom of the pool without losing contact. We often refer to these moves as "floating heads" because the head is the only body part visible above the water, yet it doesn't bounce up and down as it does during rebounding moves. One example of a neutral move is a jumping jack type of leg action. In this move, the shoulders are submerged just below the water's surface, the knees are bent, and the feet slide wide apart and then close together. This exercise is a great way to emphasize the contraction of the inner thigh muscles.

The second type of activity to avoid during your warm-up is the suspended move. As the name suggests, this type of move is performed with the body suspended in the water, without the feet touching the pool bottom. Of course, suspended moves can be done in the deep end while wearing a flotation device, but they can also be included in the exercise portion of a shallow-water workout. This type of move is very similar to treading water.

Depending on your body type, suspended moves may be either relatively easy or more intense. The more muscular your body composition, the more intensely you must work to suspend your body. The reason is simple: muscle doesn't float. In fact, muscle has high water content (about 70 percent), so you can picture muscular bodies as water balloons. And, unlike an air balloon, when you place a water balloon in the water, it sinks. Something similar happens to muscular bodies in the water, so we save suspended moves until the body is warm and can exert itself safely.

FLEXIBILITY SEGMENT

Once you complete your main workout, you should perform a cool-down—or "warm-down," as we call it in the pool, because we want you to stay warm while finishing your workout. This final segment of your workout enables your body to recover gradually from the endurance phase of your exercise. Specifically, as you slow down but continue moving, you prevent blood from pooling in your extremities. When blood pools in your extremities it does not return to your heart. If it doesn't return to your heart, then it cannot circulate to the rest of the body. If it doesn't circulate to the rest of the body, the brain may be deprived of adequate blood flow, and you might begin to feel lightheaded due to a lower blood pressure in the remainder of the body where the blood has not pooled. A moving flexibility segment will also allow your heart rate, blood pressure, and respiration rate to return to resting levels. In other words, you help your body efficiently reverse the physiological changes elicited earlier by your warm-up.

As you end your workout, your movements should become slower and smaller. One great way to gradually decrease your intensity is to return to water walking but do so at a slow, relaxing pace. You know you are decreasing the intensity if you can hold a conversation without having to stop talking to take breaths.

After water walking slowly for about three minutes, move on to a series of static stretches, which can be performed in any order. The warm-down phase is the right time for static stretching because this is when your muscles are the warmest, and warm muscles stretch more easily than cold ones. To understand this reality, think of modeling clay or any other pliable material. When such a material is left in the car on a hot day, it is much more moldable into various

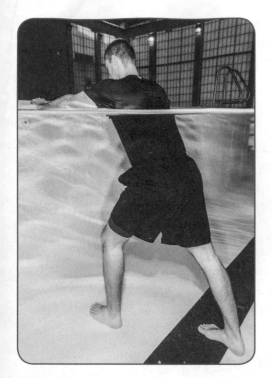

Figure 3.7 Standing calf stretch.

Figure 3.8 Standing quadriceps stretch.

shapes and lengths. However, when it is left out in the cold, it often breaks or cracks if you try to mold it. Your muscles operate in a similar manner.

To correctly perform a static stretch, take it to the point of tension and hold it without any bouncing or other movement. Hold the stretch only to the point of tightness, not discomfort or pain. Keep breathing deeply throughout the stretch. Static stretches should generally be held for 15 to 30 seconds. If you feel yourself getting cold in the water, simply move on to another muscle group or move another part of your body to keep warm.

One example of static stretching involves simply rounding your arms to the front as if you were hugging a tree, then lacing your fingers and holding the position to stretch your upper back. More static stretches are described in the following paragraphs.

For the standing calf stretch, face the side of the pool and hold on to the edge. Stand with one foot in front of the other. The distance will vary between individuals because everyone has a different level of calf flexibility. You want the feet to be far enough apart that you feel tension as you push your heel into the bottom surface of the pool. If you can keep the entire foot on the surface of the pool without feeling a stretch in the back of the lower leg (the one behind the front leg), then your legs are too close together, and you need to step the back leg back further. Bend your front knee and keep your back knee straight (see figure 3.7). Distribute your weight equally while trying to push your back heel into the bottom of the pool. Repeat with your leg position reversed.

For the standing quadriceps stretch, hold on to the edge of the pool, lift one leg behind you, bend it at the knee, and let the buoyancy of the water pull your heel to your glutes (see figure 3.8). You did a similar movement as a dynamic stretch in the warm-up phase, but now you are holding it as a static stretch. If you would like to make the stretch more intense, as your right heel is approaching your gluteus maximus (posterior hip joint), you can reach your right hand behind you and grab the arch of the right foot or the right heel and pull it to your glutes. Next, perform the same stretch on the other leg.

For the standing chest opener, you can move away from the side of the pool. Unlike the chest opener in your warm-up, you perform this one by holding your hands together behind your back and lifting them slightly (see figure 3.9). If your fingers don't touch behind your back, just keep reaching as far as you can. This is a great stretch for your chest.

For the standing side stretch, you can either stand in the middle of the pool or stand near the side and hold on to the edge. Once in position, cross your right foot in front of your left foot, extend your left arm over your head, and lean to the right (see figure 3.10). Repeat on the other side by crossing your left foot in front of your right foot, extending your right arm, and leaning to your left.

The standing hip stretch is another one that you can perform either in the middle of the pool or while holding on to the edge of the pool. If you like, you can face the pool wall, hold on to the edge with both hands, and lean back. This approach allows a deeper stretch in the hip. To perform the stretch, place one foot flat on the bottom of the pool and cross your other ankle over the knee of the weight-bearing leg. Slowly bend the knee of your standing leg to lower yourself into a chair-like position (see figure 3.11).

Figure 3.9 Standing chest opener.

Figure 3.10 Standing side stretch.

Figure 3.11 Standing hip stretch.

Now you understand why your body needs to undergo a warm-up and a warm-down with a final stretch. With this foundation in place, we can now turn our attention to the main part of the workout, which can take various forms depending on your particular needs. The following chapters describe exercises appropriate for specific rehabilitation needs and fitness levels. Let's get moving!

CHAPTER 4

BEGINNING EXERCISES

Now that you understand the benefits of water exercise and are prepared to start moving, let's introduce some basic exercises. The exercises presented in this chapter focus on the range of motion in your joints and on producing a small increase in your heart rate. The majority of these exercises do not require equipment. As you become proficient with the movements, however, you can add webbed gloves to increase the workout's intensity in order to achieve progressive overload (for more on overload, see chapter 1).

You can also achieve overload by changing your position in the pool. Almost all of the exercises presented in this chapter use a starting position in which you hold on to the edge of the pool with two hands. As you become comfortable with each exercise, you can turn to the side and hold on with only one hand (see figure 4.1). This change increases the recruitment of muscles in your core.

When it is no longer a challenge to exercise while holding on with one hand, move to the center of the pool and hold a noodle with both hands on the surface of the water. This positioning provides a balance challenge for the muscles in your core but allows you to use the noodle if you do tip forward and need to hold on to a piece of flotation equipment.

As you gradually build your confidence in the pool, move on to performing the exercises without the noodle. At first, you may feel that you don't know what to do with your arms or hands. If so, just let them move comfortably in the water. If you find that your balance is slightly off, try making small circles with your wrists and hands in the water. This movement, known as sculling, helps stabilize your core.

Figure 4.1 Turning to the side and holding the wall with only one hand increases the recruitment of your core muscles as you exercise.

The individual exercise descriptions presented in this chapter include specific safety tips, but certain safety practices apply to most exercises. The most important safety practices focus on your core, which is your powerhouse. All of the muscles in your torso act as stabilizers when you are vertical in the water. To activate your core muscles, think of tightening your core as if someone were going to punch you, and you didn't want it to hurt.

This tightening is also known as bracing, and it protects the muscles in your lower back. When your core is braced, you are less likely to injure those muscles because they are activated or working. Bracing also keeps your spinal cord in a neutral and stable position, which allows you to safely move your limbs. The stable spine also helps you keep your chest lifted, which helps you maintain your balance. In fact, these dynamics form a continuous circle: stabilizing your core improves your balance, which improves your posture, which strengthens your core.

There is no certain number of repetitions that you should perform for each exercise, but a common number to attempt is 12 repetitions with each leg or arm. Fitness research shows that 12 repetitions is the ideal number for increasing muscular endurance. If you can safely and comfortably complete 12 repetitions, the muscle fibers are no longer receiving a strong stimulus, meaning the exercise is too easy. If you can easily do 12 repetitions, you may need to add some more resistance in the form of increased surface area. You can increase your surface area with webbed gloves, fitness paddles, or water buoys. If you can only comfortably do 10 and numbers 11 and 12 are difficult, the muscle fibers are still receiving an overload (challenge). Increasing the number of repetitions is one way to achieve progressive overload in your workout, but you may have to add quite a few repetitions to fatigue the muscle and cause it to overload. The increase in repetitions may add several more minutes to your workout when you could just add more surface area to the exercise or proceed to a more advanced exercise. When you can continuously perform more than 12 reps per exercise without pain or discomfort, you can move on to the intermediate exercises presented in chapter 5. Always stop, however, if you feel pain in a joint or if you become fatigued and your form or posture suffers.

KNEE FLEXION AND EXTENSION 4.1

Equipment

None

Exercise Focus

Activates the quadriceps and hamstrings in the upper leg.

Starting Position

Stand tall with your back against the poolside and your hands gently pressed against the wall.

Action

1. Lift a straight leg naturally from the hip joint (a).
2. Bend the knee joint of the lifted leg at a right angle so that the foot drops in the water and the lower part of the leg is vertical (b).
3. From the bent-knee position, extend (straighten) the leg back to the position in step 1 (a).

Variation

As you begin to feel comfortable with the move, feel free to turn sideways and hold the wall with only one hand.

Keep It Safe

- Keep your chest lifted.
- Move the leg from the knee joint only so that the knee acts as a hinge.

4.2 HIP FLEXION

Equipment

None

Exercise Focus

Activates the hip flexors and the gluteus muscles in the hip.

Starting Position

Stand with your back to the side of the pool and your hands pressed gently against the side (a).

Action

1. With your feet together, lift one leg straight to the front as high as is comfortable (b).
2. Keeping the raised leg straight, push it down through the water to return it to the starting position (a).

Variation

As you begin to feel comfortable with the move, turn sideways and hold on to the wall with only one hand.

Keep It Safe

As the leg rises, control the lift as buoyancy tends to take over.

a

b

HIP EXTENSION 4.3

Equipment

None

Exercise Focus

Activates the hip flexors and the gluteus muscles of the hip joint.

Starting Position

With both feet flat on the pool bottom, stand facing the pool wall and gently hold on with both hands (a).

Action

1. From the hip joint, lift one leg behind you as high as is comfortable while keeping the leg straight and your hips squared toward the pool wall (b).
2. Keeping the raised leg straight, use the front of the hip joint to pull it down through the water and back to the starting position (a).

Variation

As you begin to feel comfortable with the move, turn to the side and hold on with only one hand.

4.4 LEG SWING

Equipment

None

Exercise Focus

Activates all of the muscles in the front and back of the hip and upper leg.

Starting Position

Stand sideways with one hand on the pool wall and both feet on the pool bottom.

Action

1. Using the leg that is farthest from the poolside, lift your leg to the front from the hip joint while keeping the knee as straight as possible (a).
2. When your hip feels tension in the front, immediately reverse the action and pull your leg down through the water and then behind you (b). Feel free to bend the knees slightly if it is more comfortable for your lower back.
3. When your hip feels tension in the back, immediately reverse the action and pull your leg through the water back to the front (a).

Variation

As you begin to feel comfortable with the swing, move away from the side of the pool and hold on to a noodle to challenge your balance. Hold the noodle in an overhand grip with both hands so that the noodle rests on the surface of the water.

Keep It Safe

- Move only from the hip joint.
- Keep your core stabilized.

a

b

CALF RAISE 4.5

Equipment

None

Exercise Focus

Contracts the calf muscles in the back of the lower legs.

Starting Position

With your feet shoulder-width apart on the pool bottom, face the pool wall and hold on gently with both hands (a).

Action

1. Keeping your knees straight, slowly roll onto the balls of both feet until your heels are raised as high as is comfortable (b).
2. Slowly roll your heels back down to the starting position (a).

Variation

As you begin to feel comfortable with the move, turn to the side and hold on to the pool wall with only one hand.

4.6 SQUAT

Equipment

None

Exercise Focus

Activates all of the muscles in the legs and core.

Starting Position

With your feet shoulder-width apart on the bottom of the pool, face the side of the pool and gently hold on with both hands (a).

Action

1. Gently bend your knees as you shift your weight onto your heels.
2. Continue to lower your hips either until it is no longer comfortable to do so or until your hips are level with your knees (b).
3. Pushing through your heels, straighten your knees and return to the starting position (a).

Variation

As you begin to feel comfortable with the move, turn to the side and hold on with only one hand.

Keep It Safe

- Move primarily at your knee joints; your hip joints may move slightly.
- Keep your spinal cord stable.

HIP ABDUCTION AND ADDUCTION 4.7

Equipment

None

Exercise Focus

Activates the inner and outer thigh.

Starting Position

Stand with your back to the pool wall, both hands resting gently against the poolside and both feet flat on the pool bottom.

Action

1. Keeping your toes pointed forward, lift a straight leg out to the side as high as is comfortable while keeping your hips aligned (a). Feel free to bend the knee slightly if doing so is more comfortable.
2. Keeping the raised leg straight, pull from the hip joint to move it across your support leg as far as is comfortable while keeping your hips facing forward (b).
3. Again using the hip joint, and keeping the raised leg straight, return it through the starting position and back to the first side to which you lifted it (a).

Variation

As you begin to feel comfortable with the move, turn to the side and hold on with just one hand.

Keep It Safe

Concentrate on keeping your hips and spinal cord stable.

4.8 JUMPING JACK

Equipment

None

Exercise Focus

Activates the inner and outer thighs and elevates the heart rate.

Starting Position

Face the wall with your feet together and flat on the pool bottom and with your hands gently holding on to the edge of the pool (a).

Action

1. With a small bounce or rebound, jump with both feet at the same time and land with your feet hip-width apart (b).
2. With another small bounce, jump with both feet and land with your feet back together in the beginning position (a).

Variation

When you feel comfortable with the jumping jack, move to the center of the pool and let your arms rise at your sides, stopping just short of the water level.

Keep It Safe

- As you land, be sure to roll your heels all the way to the pool bottom, both when your feet are together and when they are apart.
- When doing jumping jacks in the middle of the pool, keep your arms in the water at all times. Avoid breaking the surface of the water or lifting your arms higher than shoulder level. When you repeatedly break the surface of the water (cohesion of water molecules) with a long lever, it causes excessive stress on the active joint. In this case, when the straight arms break the surface of the water, breaking the cohesion of the water molecules can cause stress on the shoulder joint.

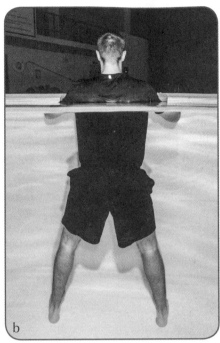

4.9 POP JUMP

Equipment

None

Exercise Focus

Activates all of the muscles in the legs and elevates the heart rate.

Starting Position

Face the wall with your feet together and flat on the pool bottom and with your hands gently holding the edge of the pool (a).

Action

1. With a small bounce, bend your knees and push your body straight up as you straighten your knees as if you were a rocket (b).
2. Return to the starting position by bending your knees gently as you land on your toes and roll all the way through to your heels (a). The knees will straighten after the starting position. The knees bend as you start your jump—a bit of momentum.

Variation

As you feel comfortable with the pop jump, move to the center of the pool and let your arms rise out to your sides, stopping just short of the water level. Jump only as high as is comfortable for you.

Keep It Safe

- As you land, be sure to roll your heels all the way to the pool bottom, with your feet together.
- When doing pop jumps in the middle of the pool, keep your arms in the water at all times. Avoid breaking the surface of the water or lifting your arms higher than shoulder level.

4.10 CROSS-COUNTRY SKI

Equipment

None

Exercise Focus

Activates the shoulder muscles and all of the muscles in the legs and core and elevates the heart rate.

Starting Position

Standing sideways by the pool wall, gently grasp the edge with one hand, and place one foot in front of the other with your feet hip-width apart (a). The arms are extended with one hand in front and one in back, opposite of the placement of the feet. If you are more comfortable holding on to the wall, gently grip the side of the pool.

Action

1. With a small bounce through a bend in the knees, push off with both feet equally and change your leg position in the air.
2. Land with both feet at the same time (b).
3. Repeat the action, reversing your leg position again, to return to the starting position (a).

Variation

As you feel comfortable performing the move by the wall, let go of the wall and move your arms in opposition to your feet.

Keep It Safe

- Keep your core stable and upright.
- Roll your feet down onto your heels after landing on your toes.

4.11 TRUNK ROTATION

Equipment

Pool noodle

Exercise Focus

Activates the external obliques of the core.

Starting Position

Stand in the middle of the pool with your feet shoulder-width apart and hold the pool noodle slightly under the surface of the water with both hands (a).

Action

1. Rotate your upper body to the right while keeping your hips forward, your feet solid on the bottom of the pool, and your spine elongated and stable. Rotate only until you feel tension in your core (b).
2. Rotate to the left (c).

Variation

Standing with your feet farther apart makes the move easier, whereas narrowing your base of support by moving your feet closer together makes the move more difficult.

Keep It Safe

- Rotate gently from your waist.
- Keep your knees softly bent.

4.12 TRICEPS PUSH-DOWN

Equipment

Pool noodle or hand buoys

Exercise Focus

Activates the triceps muscles on the back of the upper arms.

Starting Position

Stand in the middle of the pool with both feet solid on the pool bottom in either a wide stance or a split stance (with one foot slightly ahead of the other). Hold either a pool noodle or buoys on the surface of the water with an overhand grip and with bent elbows locked at your ribcage (a).

Action

1. Keeping your elbows pressed into your rib cage, straighten your arms as you push the noodle or buoys under the water (b).
2. Slowly return to the starting position by controlling the rise of the noodle or buoys (a).

Variation

If an overhand grip is uncomfortable, feel free to grasp the noodle from the underside and perform the action by pulling the noodle down instead of pushing it.

Keep It Safe

- Stabilize your core by bracing your core muscles.
- Perform the movement at your elbow joints.

BICEPS CURL 4.13

Equipment
Hand buoys or webbed gloves

Exercise Focus
Activates the biceps muscles on the front of the upper arms.

Starting Position
Stand in the middle of the pool with both feet solid on the pool bottom and your knees bent so that your shoulders are level with the surface of the water. With each hand either holding a buoy or wearing a webbed glove, extend your arms straight out to your sides just under the surface of the water (a).

Action
1. Moving at your elbow joints, bend your arms and bring the buoys or gloves to your chest (b).
2. Reverse the move by straightening your arms so that the buoys or gloves return to their starting position out to either side (a).

Variation
The biceps curl can be performed without any equipment if you find it difficult to keep the buoys or gloves under the water without elevating your shoulders.

Keep It Safe
- Stabilize your core by bracing your abdominal muscles.
- Use your elbows as hinges so that the movement occurs only in the lower portion of each arm (from your elbow to your wrist); your upper arms should be stationary.

4.14 NOODLE BICYCLE RIDING

Equipment

Pool noodle

Exercise Focus

Activates all of the muscles in the legs and core.

Starting Position

Straddling the noodle as if you were riding a horse in the middle of the pool, lower your weight onto the noodle and lift your feet off of the pool bottom so that you are floating on the noodle in an upright position (a).

Action

1. Using your hip and the knee joints, circle your legs from the front of your body to the back as if you were pedaling a bicycle.
2. As you pedal, gaze forward (b).

Variation

To add the arms as an exercise focus, use your arms as if you were swimming the freestyle stroke.

Keep It Safe

Stabilize your core by bracing your abdominal region so that you remain upright without leaning in any direction.

CHEST AND BACK OPENER 4.15

Equipment

None

Exercise Focus

Activates the muscles in the upper chest and upper back.

Starting Position

With your feet hip-width apart and staggered (one in front of the other), stabilize your core and open your arms to the back of your body as if you were stretching just after waking up in the morning (a).

Action

1. Keeping your core stabilized and moving at your shoulder joints, bring your arms through the water toward the front of your body (b).
2. After reaching the furthest point to the front, immediately reverse to open the arms to the rear of the body. Then immediately return to the front. This is a dynamic move without any holds.

Variation

This move is similar to one that you did in the warm-up, but now you can make it bigger and a bit faster, as if you were creating waves in the water. To make the exercise more of a balance challenge, stand with your feet together and move your arms at the shoulder joints. The smaller base of support makes it more difficult to stabilize your core.

Keep It Safe

Remember to move at your shoulder joints rather than through the muscles in your back.

4.16 REBOUNDING KNEE LIFT

Equipment

None

Exercise Focus

Activates the muscles in the back of the upper and lower leg.

Starting Position

Stand in the middle of the pool and be ready to give a little bounce or rebound as you lift off of one leg.

Action

1. Begin by placing the right foot on the bottom of the pool surface and letting the right knee slightly bend (a).
2. As the right knee bends, lift the left leg from the hip joint and the knee joint to the height of your hip, if possible, as you push off the right foot (b). Buoyancy and the effects of rebound will allow your body to lift, and your right foot will no longer be on the bottom of the pool.
3. As your body lowers into the water, place the left foot onto the bottom of the pool and let the left leg start to bend as the right foot now lifts from the hip and the knee joint to the height of the hip joint, if possible.

Keep It Safe

Remember that whenever you rebound in the pool, the foot that strikes the bottom of the pool needs to roll so the entire foot comes into contact with the bottom of the pool surface, and that the knee of the rebound leg will need to be slightly bent.

Variation

Once you find yourself getting into a natural rhythm, you can make your knee lifts travel forward and backward, to the right and the left, in a circle, or in a figure eight.

a   b

INTERNAL SHOULDER ROTATION 4.17

Equipment

None

Exercise Focus

Activates the four muscles comprising the shoulder's rotator cuff.

Starting Position

Stand in the middle of the pool in chest-deep water with feet firmly planted on pool bottom. Bend elbows to 90-degree angles and press them against the lower rib cage, making fists in front of the body (a).

Action

1. Keeping both elbows pressed against the ribcage, close the forearms to the midline of the torso (a).
2. Return to start.

Variation

If you feel like you are losing your balance, and would like more stability, move your feet into a split stance where feet are shoulder-width apart with one foot slightly in front of the other.

Keep It Safe

The rotator cuff muscles are small, about the size of a shoelace, so keep the movement small and listen to your body, stopping if there is pain or discomfort.

4.18 EXTERNAL SHOULDER ROTATION

Equipment

None

Exercise Focus

Activates the four muscles comprising the shoulder's rotator cuff.

Starting Position

Standing in the middle of the pool in chest-deep water with feet firmly placed on pool bottom, bend elbows to 90-degree angles and press tightly against the lower rib cage with fists in front of the body

Action

1. Press both elbows against the ribcage, open the forearms away from the midline of the torso as far as comfortable and as long as you can keep the elbows tightly against the ribcage (a).
2. Return to start.

Variation

If you feel like you are losing your balance, and would like more stability, move your feet into a split stance where feet are shoulder width apart with one foot slightly in front of the other.

Keep It Safe

The rotator cuff muscles are small, about the size of a shoelace, so keep the movement small, and listen to your body, stopping if there is pain or discomfort.

CHAPTER 5

INTERMEDIATE EXERCISES

This chapter introduces exercises that require you to be comfortable with exercising in the water. However, since they are all performed vertically, with your head above your heart, you do not need to be a swimmer in order to use them. The main difference between these exercises and the ones presented in chapter 4 is that these exercises are performed in the middle of the pool. As a result, you will not hold on to the poolside for support.

In addition, whereas the chapter 4 exercises involve only one joint, the exercises presented here involve multiple joints and therefore require you to contract more muscles. As a result, you use more muscle fibers, which requires your body to use more adenosine triphosphate (ATP)—the body's energy source—and burn more calories. Using more muscles also requires more oxygen, which causes your heart rate to increase in order to meet the greater demand.

Many of the exercises in this chapter also involve rebounding or jumping. However, if you are recovering from an injury or just starting a fitness program, remember to take it slowly at first. Specifically, start with a low number of repetitions and increase the number gradually. Jumping and rebounding require more muscular endurance and strength in the lower body than is needed for the anchored movements described in chapter 4.

As you increase the intensity of your workout, your respiration rate increases because your body uses more oxygen to help turn your fuel sources into ATP. As a result, your body attempts to take in more oxygen and give off more carbon dioxide as a waste product. As long as you continue to breathe evenly, you will be fine; avoid holding your breath, which is counterproductive. If you would like to match the rhythm of your breath to your movements, breathe out on the more difficult part of the exercise. Many people remember this rule by noting that both *exhale* and *exertion* begin with the letter E: exhale on exertion.

This chapter also includes some neutral exercises. As you may recall from chapter 3, the neutral position in the pool involves lowering your body with your knees bent, your feet in contact with the bottom of the pool, and your shoulders even with the water's surface. In this position, your feet can slide or glide along the bottom of the pool. Neutral exercises challenge your core because you are resisting the force of buoyancy, which always forces you to float to the surface. When exercising in the neutral position, it is crucial to maintain great posture; don't pull your shoulders over or let your hips stick out behind. Be sure to maintain a long, tall line through your spinal cord.

Even though this chapter offers new exercises, you begin the workout with the same warm-up exercises presented in chapter 4. The number of repetitions on each side also stays the same as before; specifically, aim for 12 repetitions with each arm or leg. Increasing the number of repetitions is one way to achieve progressive overload, and you can always increase them as long as you maintain good technique and upright posture. The posture rules also remain the same: keep your core braced, your chest lifted, your eyes on the horizon, and your shoulders down and back.

Even though chapter 5 focuses on exercises that are slightly more advanced, it does not mean that you must abandon the exercises from chapter 4. If you had some favorites in chapter 4, feel free to keep them in your workout as you proceed with the exercises from chapter 5.

STRAIGHT-LEG KICK TO THE FRONT 5.1

Equipment

None

Exercise Focus

Activates the muscles in the hip and upper leg.

Starting Position

Standing in the middle of the pool ready to rebound off of the right leg and land on one foot.

Action

1. Begin by placing the right foot on the bottom of the pool surface and letting the right knee slightly bend (a). As the right knee bends, lift the straight left leg from the hip joint to the height of your hip if possible as you push off the right foot. Buoyancy and the rebound will allow your body to lift and your right foot will no longer be on the bottom of the pool.

2. As your body lowers into the water, land on the bottom of the pool with the left foot and let the left leg start to bend as the right foot now lifts from the hip height of the hip joint if possible (b).

3. As you begin to lower into the water, land on the right foot on the bottom of the pool with a slight knee bend so you can rebound and begin step 1 again.

Variation

To increase the intensity, travel either forward and backward or to the right or left as you kick.

Keep It Safe

Remember that every time your foot strikes the bottom of the pool to rebound, you need to bend the knee and roll the entire foot down onto the bottom of the pool.

5.2 ROCKING HORSE

Equipment

None

Exercise Focus

Provides a whole-body workout.

Starting Position

Standing in the middle of the pool ready to rebound forward onto one leg.

Action

1. As you rebound forward onto your right foot, landing with a soft knee, pull your arms around as if you were hugging a tree, while your left back heel rises towards your glutes (a).
2. With a small rebound, transfer your weight to your back foot as your arms open up to stretch your chest and your front right knee lifts to hip level if possible (b).
3. Rebound forward to your front leg and repeat.

Variation

If the arm movements seem difficult, bend your elbows as you rock forward and do a biceps curl. As you rock backward, straighten your elbow joints.

Keep It Safe

Make sure your heels roll completely to the pool bottom on every rocking horse repetition.

SIDE MOGUL 5.3

Equipment

None

Exercise Focus

Activates the muscles in the legs and core.

Starting Position

Standing in the middle of the pool with your feet together.

Action

1. Push off of the pool bottom with your feet together and your hips forward, then land with your feet together and slightly to the right side of your starting point (a).
2. Immediately push off with both feet and return to the starting position to the left side of the starting position (b).

Variation

To increase the intensity of the mogul, pull your knees up into a tucked position on each jump as you move from side to side.

Keep It Safe

Land with both feet at the same time and on the balls of your feet, then roll through to your heels.

5.4 TWISTING MOGUL

Equipment

None

Exercise Focus

Activates all of the muscles in the legs and core.

Starting Position

Standing in the middle of the pool with your feet together (a).

Action

1. As you bend your knees to push off with feet from the starting position, rotate your body to the right side and land with both feet together at a slight 45-degree angle (b).

2. Pushing off of both feet, rotate your body to the left side, landing on both feet while slightly facing the left side at a 45-degree angle.

Variation

To increase the intensity of the exercise, pull your knees up into a tucked position after each push-off, then straighten them as you land facing the opposite side.

Keep It Safe

Land on the balls of your feet and roll all the way down onto your heels.

PENDULUM 5.5

Equipment

None

Exercise Focus

Activates the inner and outer thigh muscles.

Starting Position

Standing in the middle of the pool with all of your weight on one leg and with your other leg extended out to the side. Your arms should reach out on the same side as your loaded (weight-bearing) leg (a).

Action

1. Giving a small push or rebounding off of your loaded leg, swing your extended leg in to touch your loaded leg.
2. Your loaded leg now becomes your extended leg as your arms swing through the water to the same side as your new loaded leg. Your movement should mimic the back-and-forth action of a pendulum (b).

Variation

To increase the workout for your core muscles, hold your arms still just barely under the water and straight out to the side. This position forces your torso muscles to stabilize you so that you remain upright.

Keep It Safe

Make sure that your legs touch in the middle of the movement. Think of clicking your heels right before your weight shifts.

a

b

5.6 SOCCER KICK

Equipment

None

Exercise Focus

Activates all of the muscles in the legs and core.

Starting Position

Standing in the middle of the pool ready to rebound forward onto one leg as your other leg swings back as if to start a kick.

Action

1. Let your free leg swing back as your weight shifts forward onto your support leg. Your torso should lean slightly forward (a).
2. Swing your back leg through so that it kicks forward and you lean slightly backward (b).
3. Land on your front leg as the previously loaded leg swings back for a kick.

Keep It Safe

Let your leg swing behind and slightly to the side so that when you kick through, the final kick clears the body as it moves forward. As the foot of your support leg contacts the pool bottom, land on your toes and roll your heel all the way to the bottom.

a

b

HOEDOWN KICK 5.7

Equipment

None

Exercise Focus

Activates all of the muscles in the legs and core.

Starting Position

Stand in the middle of the pool ready to rebound onto one foot.

Action

1. As you rebound onto your left foot, lift the right bent knee to hip height, if possible, keeping both the hip and knee joints bent.
2. Immediately after you have lifted the right leg with the hip joint and knee joint bent, straighten the knee joint.
3. After straightening the knee joint, lower the right leg so that the right foot makes contact with the pool bottom, and rebound off the right foot, while lifting the left leg to hip height with the knee and the hip joint bent. As soon as the left leg is lifted, straighten out the knee joint and return the left leg to the pool bottom ready to repeat the entire process.

Variation

You can incorporate your arms into the workout, as seen in the photos. As you lift a leg, hold your hands close together and push them down to the middle of the body. As you switch feet, let your arms return to chest level.

Keep It Safe

Land first on your toes, then let your heels roll down.

5.8 REAR KICK

Equipment

None

Exercise Focus

Activates the muscles in the legs and core.

Starting Position

Standing in the middle of the pool with your core stabilized, ready to jump onto one foot.

Action

1. Rebound forward onto your right foot. As your right foot strikes the pool surface and the knee bends slightly, lift your straight left leg to the rear as high as possible. Keep it as straight as you can and push both arms straight in front of your body (a).

2. As your left foot lowers, place it on the bottom of the pool as the knee slightly bends. Rebound while lifting your straight right leg behind you as high as possible, while keeping it straight as you push both arms straight in front of you (b).

Variation

To increase the intensity of the exercise, move your body either forward and backward or to either side as you kick backward. For example, alternate back kicks for four rebounds as you move your body across the pool. Then keep alternating and return the way you came.

Keep It Safe

If you feel discomfort in your back when kicking with a straight leg, feel free to bend slightly at the knee joint.

5.9 CRISS-CROSS JUMPING JACK

Equipment

None

Exercise Focus

Activates the inner and outer thighs, as well as the muscles surrounding the shoulder joints.

Starting Position

Stand in the middle of the pool with your feet together on the pool bottom, ready to jump and move your feet apart.

Action

1. With your legs remaining straight, give a bounce or a small rebound off of the pool bottom, then land with your feet shoulder-width apart and your arms extended straight out to the sides at shoulder height, which should be right at the water's surface (a).

2. As you jump, bring your feet back together and let one foot cross behind the other as your arms come down in front of your body and cross at the wrists or forearms (b).

3. Push off again and return to the shoulder-width stance with arms extended out to the sides (a).

4. Jump again and bring your feet back together, but this time cross the other foot behind with arms crossed front.

Variation

It is a bit more intense, but still relatively easy, to perform criss-cross jacks while moving to either side. It is much more difficult, however, to perform them while moving forward and backward, which requires you to lead with greater surface area.

Keep It Safe

- If keeping your arms straight is uncomfortable to your shoulder joints, feel free to bend slightly at the elbow joints and omit crossing at the wrist.
- Always keep your arms in the water—unlike doing jacks on land, your arms should never go above your head.

5.10 STAR JACK

Equipment

None

Exercise Focus

Activates all of the muscles in the legs, arms, and core.

Starting Position

Stand in the middle of the pool with both feet on the pool bottom (a) ready to rebound with a small bounce onto one leg.

Action

1. As you rebound by pushing off the pool bottom, pull your legs apart and lift your left leg slightly to the side, then land on your right leg. As you land, let your right arm continue up to about eye level and keep your left arm low in the water (b).
2. Push off with your right leg, on which you just landed, and return to the starting position (a).
3. Reverse by pushing with your left foot as your left arm goes slightly above your shoulders to eye level, then return to the starting position with both feet together (a).

Keep It Safe

If it feels uncomfortable to keep your arm straight as you lift it out of the water, feel free to bend it at the elbow to make it a shorter lever (see chapter 1) as it comes out of the water.

TUCK JUMP 5.11

Equipment

None (pool noodle optional)

Exercise Focus

Activates the muscles in the core and surrounding the hip joints.

Starting Position

Stand in the middle of the pool with your toes lightly touching the bottom and your knees bent so that your shoulders are even with the water's surface (a).

Action

1. Bracing your core and your knees together, tuck both knees slowly and tightly into your chest (b).
2. Slowly return to the starting position (a).

Variation

If you are uncomfortable in the water with your knees bent and nothing but your head above the surface, wrap a noodle around your waist and hold on to the ends of the noodle.

Keep It Safe

This exercise focuses on the muscles in your core, so it is important for you to engage or activate the muscles of your trunk and move only from your hip joints. Your tucking motion should be slow and controlled.

a

b

5.12 FRONT-TO-BACK MOGUL

Equipment

None

Exercise Focus

Activates all of the muscles in your arms, legs, and core.

Starting Position

Stand in the middle of the pool with both feet on the pool bottom. If the pool has lane lines, you can use one of them as a target to jump over.

Action

1. Bend your knees, give a small bounce or rebound to lift both feet at the same time, and jump over the lane line or an imaginary line (a). As you propel yourself off the bottom of the pool, use your arms by starting them in the front and landing with them behind you (as if you were a downhill skier).

2. As soon as you touch down in front of the line, reverse everything and jump backward. This time, your arms move from a position slightly behind your hips to one in front of your hips (b).

Keep It Safe

Brace your core and bend your knees to create a solid, powerful push.

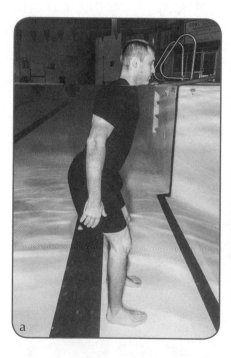

NEUTRAL JACK 5.13

Equipment

None

Exercise Focus

Activates the muscles of the inner and outer thighs and the core.

Starting Position

Standing in the middle of the pool with your feet together and your knees bent so that you are submerged to your shoulders (a).

Action

1. Keeping your feet in contact with the pool bottom, use your outer thighs to slide your feet out as far apart as is comfortable (b).
2. Keeping your feet in contact with the bottom, use your inner thighs to return your legs to the starting position (a).

Variation

Try increasing the speed of your movement to produce greater recruitment of muscle fibers in your inner and outer thighs.

5.14 NEUTRAL CROSS-COUNTRY

Equipment

None

Exercise Focus

Activates all of the muscles in your arms, legs, core, and back.

Starting Position

Standing in the middle of the pool in a largely submerged position so that your shoulders blades are even with the surface of the water.

Action

1. Extend one leg to the front, along with the opposite arm, and extend the other leg and other arm behind you.
2. While keeping your feet in contact with the bottom, slide your feet and reverse your leg and arm positions. This move is very similar to cross-country skiing, except you are doing this cross-country skiing in place.

Variation

To increase the intensity of the exercise, add a double-leg tuck in the middle of the move: extend, tuck, extend.

HURDLE LEAP 5.15

Equipment

None

Exercise Focus

Activates the muscles in the legs and core.

Starting Position

Stand in the middle of the pool with one foot lifted (a). Be ready to rebound and propel the body forward.

Action

1. As you push off with your back (support) foot, straighten your front knee joint (b).
2. Land on the front leg with the knee gently bent. The rear leg will be slightly bent (c).
3. Swing the rear leg through to the front of the body and reverse on the other side.

Keep It Safe

As you propel your body, use your arms in the water by pulling them from front to back to help you move forward.

5.16 CARIOCA

Equipment

None

Exercise Focus

Activates all of the muscles in your legs, hips, and core.

Starting Position

Stand in the middle of the pool so that you have room to move both to the right and to the left. Hold your arms chest high, extended to each side.

Action

1. Take a normal side step to the right with your right leg.
2. Cross your left leg behind your right leg and let your arms move naturally (a).
3. Take another normal side step to the right with your right leg (b).
4. Cross your left leg in front of your right leg and let your arms move naturally (c).
5. Let your arms move naturally, as you would if doing this exercise on land.
6. Continue in this manner until you are no longer in chest-deep water or have no room left to move. Then repeat in the other direction.

Keep It Safe

Keep your hips and shoulders squared to the front. If your lower body is inflexible, start with small steps. Over time, you will be able to take longer steps.

5.17 SERPENTINE RUNNING

Equipment

None

Exercise Focus

Focuses on balance and on the cardiovascular system.

Starting Position

Stand in chest-deep water with room to move forward.

Action

1. Run in a zigzag pattern as if you were weaving through an obstacle course of cones.
2. When you get to the side of the pool, turn around and repeat by running in a serpentine pattern as if you were weaving through an obstacle course of cones.

Variation

To increase the intensity, start by running in a zigzag fashion, but on your return trip, run straight back through the zigzag current that you just created.

ANCHORED JAB PUNCH 5.18

Equipment

None

Exercise Focus

Focuses on the upper body.

Starting Position

Stand in the middle of the pool with your feet grounded on the pool bottom and positioned shoulder-width apart.

Action

1. Keeping your feet anchored and your core tight, use your upper back to start a rotation into a punch directly in front of you.
2. When the elbow of your punching arm is just short of straight, return to the starting position and jab with your other arm.

Variation

The more quickly you throw your punches, the more intense the exercise will be. You can add buoys by holding one in each hand if you are working to increase muscular strength and endurance in your upper body.

5.19 ANCHORED ARM CHAOS

Equipment

None

Exercise Focus

Focuses on the upper body.

Starting Position

Stand in the middle of the pool with your feet anchored on the pool bottom and positioned shoulder-width apart.

Action

1. With elbows slightly bent, extend arms to the front at chest level. Open your fingers and slightly cup your hands.
2. Keeping your fingers wide and your hands cupped, rotate your hands around each other as quickly as you can, as if you were trying to pull all of the water into your chest.
3. Continue for as long as you can (until your upper body fatigues).

Variation

To make the exercise less intense, close your fingers. To increase the intensity, keep your fingers wide and rotate your hands around each other for a longer time. You can also increase the intensity by adding webbed gloves if you are working to increase muscular strength and endurance in your arms.

SIDE SQUAT 5.20

Equipment

None

Exercise Focus

Activates all of the muscles in the legs.

Starting Position

Stand in the middle of the pool with room to move to the right and the left (a).

Action

1. Starting with your right foot, step comfortably wide as you bend from the knee joint (b). This is not a rebounding or jumping move. It is an anchored or grounded move, which means that you should always have at least one foot in contact with the pool bottom.

2. Straighten both knees at the same time as you push upward from both feet. Reverse in the opposite direction.

Variation

Feel free to vary the width of your side step. If you have tight hip joints, start small and gradually increase the length of your step.

Keep It Safe

Always keep your chest lifted and your eyes on the horizon. If you find yourself bending forward, your side step is too wide.

a

b

5.21 WALKING LUNGE

Equipment

None

Exercise Focus

Activates all of the muscles in the legs and core.

Starting Position

With your hands on your hips, stand in chest-deep water where you have room to move forward with at least one foot anchored to the ground at all times (a).

Action

1. Take a step forward and bend each knee to a 90-degree angle while keeping your chest directly over your hips (b).
2. Push off of your back foot and return your feet to the starting position (a).
3. Repeat by stepping forward with your other leg.

Keep It Safe

If your chest drops as you step forward, try taking a smaller step and bending your knees less. As your hips become more flexible, you will be able to take larger steps and remain upright.

STRAIGHT-LEG ZOMBIE WALK 5.22

Equipment

None

Exercise Focus

Activates the muscles of the hip joints and core.

Starting Position

Stand in chest-deep water where you have room to move forward with at least one foot anchored to the bottom of the pool (a).

Action

1. Keeping one foot in contact with the pool bottom at all times, slowly control a front-leg lift while keeping your knee joint straight but not locked (b).
2. Let buoyancy pull your leg up as far as you find comfortable while maintaining proper posture.
3. Return the raised leg to the starting position (a) and perform the lift with the other leg.

Variation

You can let your arms move naturally or try to touch the toes of the lifted leg with the opposite hand.

Keep It Safe

If you find yourself bending forward at the hips when you lift your leg, start with a lower height. Your chest should remain directly above your hip joints.

5.23 TIGHTROPE TRAVELING

Equipment

None

Exercise Focus

Focuses on balance.

Starting Position

Stand in chest-deep water with room to move forward. If you are in a lap pool, stand on a lane line with one foot in front of the other and both feet on the line; otherwise, use an imaginary line.

Action

1. Hold your arms out to the side as if you were a tightrope walker.
2. Place one foot in front of the other as you walk in a straight line.

Variation

For a different balance challenge, try going backward.

LATERAL TRUNK FLEXION 5.24

Equipment

Buoy or pool noodle

Exercise Focus

Activates the core muscles.

Starting Position

Stand in the middle of the pool in chest-deep water with your feet anchored on the pool bottom, your right arm hanging to your right side, your right hand holding the noodle or buoy, and your left hand on your hip or hanging by your left side (a).

Action

1. Brace your core, keep your chest lifted, and push the noodle into the water while keeping your elbow straight but not locked (b).
2. When you can no longer maintain proper posture while lowering the noodle, return to the starting position.

Variation

The exercise is easier if your feet are farther apart; it is more intense if you stand with your feet side by side.

5.25 SINGLE-LEG PRESS

Equipment

Pool noodle

Exercise Focus

Activates all of the muscles in the legs and core.

Starting Position

Stand in the middle of the pool. Hold the ends of the noodle with your hands and use the arch of one foot to hold the middle of the noodle down, allowing it to form a U shape (a). Your other foot should remain anchored to the bottom of the pool throughout the exercise.

Action

1. Hold the ends of the noodle with a comfortable grip.
2. Keeping your chest lifted, hold the noodle, straighten your bent knee, and use that foot to push the noodle down until your arms are straight (b).
3. Slowly return to the starting position (a).

CHEST PRESS 5.26

Equipment

Pool noodle or two buoys

Exercise Focus

Activates the upper chest and back.

Starting Position

Stand in chest-deep water in a split stance, feet shoulder-distance apart with one foot behind the other. Using an overhand grip, hold close to your chest either a pool noodle in both hands or a buoy in each hand (a).

Action

1. Keeping the equipment just under the surface of the water, extend your elbow joints to push the equipment through the water. Stop when your elbows are straight but not locked (b).
2. Return to the starting position by bending your elbows and pulling the equipment back through the water to your chest (a).

Variation

If you are using buoys, you can alternate arms rather than moving them together. Alternating gives one chest muscle the chance to rest while you work the other. Unilateral (one side and then the other) work will always be easier than bilateral (both sides together) work.

Keep It Safe

Keep your core braced and your feet anchored on the pool bottom so that you use your upper body and not your hip joints.

5.27 STRAIGHT-ARM PUSH-DOWN

Equipment

Pool noodle

Exercise Focus

Activates the muscles in the upper torso surrounding the spine and the shoulder joints.

Starting Position

Stand in the middle of the pool with your feet shoulder-width apart.

Action

1. Stabilize your core and let the noodle rise to the water's surface while holding it in a loose overhand grip with both hands and with your arms straight (a).
2. Keeping your arms straight throughout the movement, push through your upper back to lower the noodle until it touches your thighs (b).
3. Control the noodle as you let it rise slowly back to the starting position (a).

Variation

If you have access to water buoys, you can use them instead of a noodle by holding one in each hand with an overhand grip. You can push them down either at the same time or in alternating fashion.

Keep It Safe

Even though your arms are straight, your elbow joints should remain soft; in other words, avoid locking them out with completely straight arms.

HORIZONTAL SHOULDER 5.28
ABDUCTION AND ADDUCTION

Equipment

None

Exercise Focus

Activates the muscles of the shoulder joints.

Starting Position

Stand in the middle of the pool in chest-deep water with your arms straight out to your sides, your thumbs up, and your feet together (a).

Action

1. Using both arms at the same time, bring your arms to the front until they meet; keep your elbows straight throughout the movement (b).
2. Return to the starting position (a).

Variation

To decrease the intensity of the exercise, start with your palms facing down and retain that hand position as you move through the full range of motion. To increase the intensity, use webbed gloves or hold a buoy in each hand; if you use this approach, make sure that the equipment stays in the water as you move through the full range of motion.

5.29 WALL PUSH-UP

Equipment

None

Exercise Focus

Activates the muscles in your upper body and core.

Starting Position

Stand by the side of the pool, leaning slightly into the pool edge, with your hands slightly wider than chest-width apart, and press them against either the poolside or a ledge inside the pool (a).

Action

1. Shift your weight into your arms as you slowly lean forward and lower your body toward the side of the pool (b). As you slowly shift your weight and lean forward, you may feel more comfortable to lift onto your toes.
2. When the bend in your elbow joints makes a right angle, exhale and push your body back to the starting position (a).

Variation

To increase the intensity of the exercise, position your feet farther from the wall so that your arms bear more of your body weight. To challenge your balance, lift one leg slightly off of the pool bottom.

Keep It Safe

Brace your core so that your back stays in a neutral position—no arching or rounding.

PRONE HIP ABDUCTION 5.30
AND ADDUCTION

Equipment

None

Exercise Focus

Activates the core and the inner and outer thighs.

Starting Position

Face the side of the pool and gently grasp it. Hold your legs together and extend them straight behind you. You will be floating on the front side of your body (a). Depending on the composition of your body, whether you carry more fat mass or lean-tissue mass, you may float to the top or feel your body slightly submerged as you see in the photo.

Action

1. Keeping your core braced and using only a light grasp on the poolside, open your legs into a straddle position as far as you find comfortable (b).
2. Return to the starting position by pulling your legs through the water and back together (a).

Keep It Safe

If your hips pop out of the water as you move your legs apart, try decreasing your range of motion. As your flexibility increases, you will be able to move through a greater range of motion without letting your hips lift out of the water.

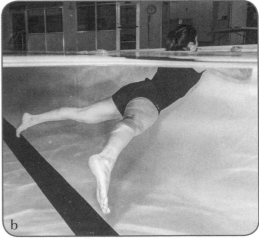

CHAPTER 6

ADVANCED EXERCISES

This chapter presents exercises that activate multiple muscle groups and challenge your balance. These exercises often require the activation of your upper body, lower body, and core. Whenever your core is challenged, you also improve your balance, which decreases your risk of falls, increases your enjoyment of daily life activities, and improves your sport skills.

By the time you have progressed to these advanced exercises, you should be fairly comfortable in the water. These exercises include some rebounding moves and several suspended moves, which require you to lift both feet off the bottom of the pool at the same time. To help you stay afloat, you will need to scull your hands out to the side of your body. Whenever you feel the need to take a break, you can tap down on the bottom of the pool. Start with a goal of going 8 to 10 seconds without a break and gradually increase to 30 seconds.

This chapter also includes some flotation exercises, which require you to use a pool noodle—often by wrapping the noodle around your back so that you can hold its ends in your hands. These flotation exercises focus mainly on core stability, so slow your speed when performing them and concentrate on bracing your core. This bracing activates the posterior wall of your trunk, which supports proper posture, as well as the anterior abdominal wall, which also helps hold you upright. Contracting these muscles concurrently helps protect you from injury or reinjury. If the wall is not braced, you are more likely to be injured because the muscle is not activated to support surrounding structures such as your spinal cord. If you are working in a shallow pool, this chapter concludes the basic exercises appropriate for you. Chapter 7 introduces deep-water exercises, and the remaining chapters present programs for specific joints and populations.

6.1 FROG JUMP

Equipment

None

Exercise Focus

Activates the muscles in the legs and core.

Starting Position

Stand in the middle of the pool with your feet turned slightly out and be ready to rebound off of two feet (a).

Action

1. Push off of the bottom of the pool and open your hip joints so that your knees point out to your sides as you lift your feet toward your groin. Simultaneously, push both hands down between your legs so that you resemble a leaping frog (b).
2. Land safely on both feet (a) and repeat.

Keep It Safe

When landing, always roll down onto your heels after initially landing on your toes.

CROOKED JACK 6.2

Equipment

None

Exercise Focus

Activates the muscles in your legs and core with a focus on balance.

Starting Position

Stand in the middle of the pool on both feet (a) and be ready to rebound off of the pool bottom.

Action

1. Rebound off of both feet and spread your feet apart as if doing a jumping jack, but land only on your right foot. Lean slightly to the right and keep your left foot elevated above the pool bottom. Drop your right arm into the water and raise your left arm level to the water's surface, forming a straight line with your right arm (b).

2. Rebound off of your right foot and return to the starting position (a), then perform the exercise on your left side.

Keep It Safe

To allow yourself to get comfortable with the exercise, start with just a slight lean. As your balance improves, you can lean a bit more.

6.3 SIDE LEAP

Equipment

None

Exercise Focus

Activates muscles throughout the body.

Starting Position

Stand in the middle of the pool, support all of your weight on your left leg, bend your right leg at the knee, and position its foot beside the knee of your supporting left leg (a). Be ready to bounce or rebound to the right side while extending your right knee into a straightened position. The arms will be used to pull the water to the left, so begin with your right arm extended straight out to the right side and the left arm extended across your body to the right side.

Action

1. Push off with the foot of your support leg (left leg as pictured), extend your bent leg (right) sideways, and leap sideways to land on the now-extended right leg with a slightly bent knee (b). Facilitate your motion by pulling your arms through the water to the left side.

2. The lifted left leg now steps back in to return you to the starting position (a), from which you can repeat the movement.

Keep It Safe

If your hip joints are tight, start with small leaps. As you become more flexible, you can increase your range of motion.

POWER JACK 6.4

Equipment

None

Exercise Focus

Focuses on the heart and the leg muscles.

Starting Position

Stand in the middle of the pool with your feet together (a) and be ready to jump up into a tuck position.

Action

1. Jump up into the tuck position, tightening the muscles in your core as you jump (b).
2. From the tuck position, spread your legs to land with your feet shoulder-width apart as in a jumping jack (c).
3. Immediately push off and tuck again (b) before landing back in the starting position (a), from which you will repeat the sequence.

Variation

This exercise should be challenging, but if you find that you need more muscle recruitment, try moving the power jacks forward and backward in the pool.

Keep It Safe

This is an intense exercise that greatly increases your heart rate. Start slowly and gradually increase your repetitions and speed.

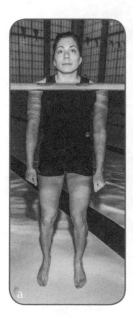

6.5 ROCKET

Equipment

None

Exercise Focus

Focuses on the heart and the leg muscles.

Starting Position

Stand in the middle of the pool with your feet shoulder-width apart, arms stretched out to your sides (a), ready to jump.

Action

1. Push off with both feet simultaneously and shoot straight into the air as you pull your straight legs together, pulling your arms together in front of your body (b).
2. Return to the starting position (a) and repeat the movement.

Keep It Safe

This is an intense exercise that greatly increases your heart rate. Start slowly and gradually increase your repetitions and speed.

REBOUNDING LEG SWING 6.6

Equipment

None

Exercise Focus

Activates the muscles in the legs and core.

Starting Position

Stand in the middle of the pool on your left foot and be ready to rebound.

Action

1. Swing your right leg to the front and rebound off of your left foot so that you are lifted in the water (a).
2. Swing your right leg back to the center and let it continue to the back (b). As your right leg passes through, your left leg will rebound off of the pool surface again so you can swing through.

Variation

To increase the intensity of the exercise, make your body travel forward and backward through the water as you swing. To greatly increase the intensity, keep your hips squared to the front and travel to the right and left.

Keep It Safe

If swinging with a straight leg is uncomfortable for your lower back, feel free to slightly bend your swinging leg.

6.7 SUSPENDED JACK

Equipment

None

Exercise Focus

Activates the muscles in the legs and core.

Starting Position

Stand in the middle of the pool with your feet shoulder-width apart and be ready to move into a suspended position.

Action

1. Lift your feet and move them apart (move each out to the side), then remain suspended in the water as you alternate between moving your feet together and moving them apart. To remain suspended, scull (make small circles) with your arms out to your sides.

2. Continue to scull and move your legs as the motion of the water around your body holds you up. Gradually try to increase your action time to 30 seconds.

Keep It Safe

The more muscle contained in your body mass, the faster you will have to move your arms and legs to stay afloat.

SUSPENDED EGGBEATER 6.8

Equipment

None

Exercise Focus

Activates the muscles in the legs and core.

Starting Position

Stand in the middle of the pool with your feet shoulder-width apart and be ready to move into a suspended position.

Action

1. Lift both feet out, each to its own side, and circle one leg clockwise and the other leg counterclockwise as you stay suspended. To remain suspended, you will need to scull with your arms out to your sides.
2. Your leg motions should continue in opposite directions to resemble the action of an eggbeater.
3. Continue to scull and move your legs as the motion of the water around your body holds you up. Gradually try to increase your action time to 30 seconds.

6.9 DOUBLE-LEG PUSH-DOWN

Equipment

Pool noodle

Exercise Focus

Activates the muscles in the legs and core.

Starting Position

Stand on the noodle with your arches pressing down into it (a). The noodle will be on the bottom of the pool, and your body weight will be holding it down.

Action

1. Engage your core and control the noodle as you bend your knees into your chest to assume a tuck position. You have a choice of arm positions—either gently sculling the water (b) or gently holding the ends of the noodle.

2. Control the noodle with your legs, keeping your core engaged, as you straighten your legs back out as far as comfortable with the noodle still under your feet (a).

SIDE SHOOT-THROUGH 6.10

Equipment

Pool noodle

Exercise Focus

Activates the core muscles.

Starting Position

Wrap the pool noodle around your upper back, hold on to its ends with your hands in front of you, holding on to an end of the noodle with each hand, and tuck into a neutral position with your toes slightly off the bottom of the pool (a).

Action

1. Contract your abdominal muscles, pull your knees into a tighter tuck, and then lean your upper body slightly to the left as you straighten your legs and extend them to your right. Keep your legs positioned tightly together (b).

2. Return to the tuck position (a) and then extend to the opposite side. Your motion should be slow and controlled as you perform a tight tuck that extends into a long stretch.

Variation

When just starting this exercise, feel free to allow your toes to barely touch the bottom as you extend. Once you are more comfortable with the move, extend without letting your toes touch the bottom of the pool.

6.11 FRONT AND BACK SHOOT-THROUGH

Equipment

Pool noodle

Exercise Focus

Activates the core muscles.

Starting Position

Wrap the pool noodle around your upper back, holding each end of the noodle and tuck into a neutral position with your toes slightly off the bottom of the pool (a).

Action

1. Contract your abdominal muscles, pull your knees into a tighter tuck, and then lean your upper body slightly to the front as you straighten your legs and extend them to the rear. Keep your legs positioned tightly together (b).

2. Return to the tuck position (a), then extend your legs to the front as your body tilts slightly backward. Your motion should be slow and controlled as you perform a tight tuck that extends into a long stretch (c).

Variation

When just starting this exercise, feel free to allow your toes to barely touch bottom when extending the legs to the front and the back. Once you are more comfortable with the move, extend without letting your toes touch the bottom of the pool.

6.12 FLOTATION EXTENSION AND ABDUCTION-ADDUCTION

Equipment

Pool noodle

Exercise Focus

Activates the muscles in the legs and core.

Starting Position

Wrap the noodle around your upper back, hold on to its ends with your hands in front of you holding one end of the noodle with each hand. Tuck into a neutral position with your toes off the bottom of the pool (a).

Action

1. As you lift your toes from the bottom of the pool, straighten your knee joints and let your legs extend in front of you at a right angle to your body (b).
2. Maintaining the right angle with your legs, open them into a wide straddle position (c).
3. Return to the extended position (b), then bend your knees back to the starting position (a), from which you can repeat the sequence.

Variation

This is a two-stage exercise. Begin by doing only the tuck and extension. Once you have become proficient, add the V-sit as seen in the final photograph (c).

6.13 NOODLE BALANCE

Equipment

Pool noodle

Exercise Focus

Activates the core muscles.

Starting Position

Stand in the middle of the pool with the noodle captured underneath both feet on the bottom of the pool.

Action

Activate your core muscles and experiment with moving your feet to various positions while maintaining your balance. To help you maintain your balance, let your arms extend out to the side or in front of you.

Variation

Positioning your feet in a wider base of support makes the exercise easier, whereas positioning them side by side intensifies the balance challenge.

Keep It Safe

When you are finished, slowly lift one foot from the noodle at a time to avoid having the noodle hit you in the face. Once one end of the noodle rises to the water's surface, you can grab it.

STATIONARY PLANK 6.14

Equipment

Pool noodle

Exercise Focus

Activates the core muscles.

Starting Position

Hold the noodle with both hands in an overhand grip, lean slightly into the water, and slowly walk your feet out behind you until your body forms a long diagonal line from your shoulders to your heels.

Action

Let your toes lightly touch the bottom of the pool as you continue to balance in this position. To increase your stability, keep the noodle almost directly beneath your shoulder joints. Gradually try to increase your balancing time to 30 seconds.

Variation

Once you become proficient at holding this plank position, lift one foot slightly (two inches, or about five centimeters) and hold the position with only your other foot touching the bottom.

Keep It Safe

Let your body lean forward as a unit and keep your neck in a neutral position as you gaze toward the pool bottom.

6.15 SIDE NOODLE PLANK

Equipment

Pool noodle

Exercise Focus

Activates the core muscles.

Starting Position

Stand on the pool floor and lean sideways until your body is positioned in an incline. Your head should remain out of the water and in a neutral position with your eyes gazing straight ahead. Hold the noodle in your bottom hand directly below your shoulder.

Action

With your hips stacked on top of each other and your body aligned from toes to shoulders, hold the position for 30 seconds, then switch sides.

Variation

When the move is no longer challenging, stabilize your core as you slowly lift your top leg about 12 inches (30 centimeters) and then reset it on your bottom leg.

PLANK SCULLING 6.16

Equipment

None

Exercise Focus

Activates the core muscles.

Starting Position

Stand on the pool floor and lean forward until your body is positioned on an incline. Your head should remain out of the water and in a neutral position with your eyes gazing down into the water.

Action

Scull the water with your hands as if you were treading water. Try to maintain your stable diagonal position for 30 seconds while sculling.

Variation

When this move is no longer challenging, lift one foot slightly and tread with just the other foot on the bottom of the pool surface.

6.17 SIDE-BALANCE LEAN

Equipment

None

Exercise Focus

Focuses on balance and on the core.

Starting Position

Stand with your feet anchored on the pool bottom. Be ready to lift one leg and assume a leaning position where you lift one leg slightly out to the side and balance. Your arms can be placed wherever they are comfortable to help keep the balance.

Action

Shift your weight onto your right foot, lift your left leg, and drop your right arm. Your left arm should form a diagonal line along with your right arm. Gradually increase your balance time to 30 seconds on each side.

Variation

To increase the difficulty of the move, have a partner create turbulence around your balance pose. You can also increase the challenge by sharing pool space with children as they jump and splash around.

TRICEPS PUSH-UP 6.18

Equipment

None

Exercise Focus

Activates the tricep, the small muscle in the back of the arm.

Starting Position

Face the side of the pool and lean against it with your arms braced shoulder-width apart (a).

Action

1. Keeping your elbows in toward your body, shift your weight forward and lean into your arms as you bend your elbows (b).
2. Straighten your elbows as you return to the starting position (a).

Variation

To increase the challenge, lift one foot slightly away from the pool bottom; this change activates your core.

6.19 SPIDERMAN CRAWL

Equipment

None

Exercise Focus

Activates muscles throughout the body.

Starting Position

Face the side of the pool. Hold on to it with your arms braced shoulder-width apart and lean away from the wall (a). Your feet will be touching the wall near the bottom of the pool.

Action

1. Keeping your upper body in place, bend your knees and climb up the wall one step at a time (b). As your feet get closer to your hands, your hips will protrude behind you.

2. When you reach the top, reverse and slowly step your feet down the wall toward the pool bottom.

WOOD CHOP **6.20**

Equipment

None

Exercise Focus

Activates muscles throughout the body.

Starting Position

In chest-deep water with both feet planted firmly on the pool bottom, place your arms straight and your palms together in front of your body, then lift them overhead to the right side of your body (a).

Action

1. With a powerful straight-arm sweep, cut across your body and into the water (b).
2. Without the powerful stroke, return to the starting position (a) and repeat the movement.

Variation

To increase the balance challenge, move your feet closer together. To decrease the challenge, widen your stance.

Keep It Safe

If your shoulder joints are uncomfortable as your arms enter the water, shorten the lever (see chapter 1) by bending your elbows slightly.

CHAPTER 7

DEEP-WATER EXERCISES

When you exercise in deep water, your options are limited by the fact that your feet cannot touch the bottom of the pool with your head above the water. As a result, you cannot perform rebounding, anchored, or neutral exercises. Instead, you must use flotation positions, and a flotation device is needed. The two best options are the pool noodle and the flotation belt. The noodle is a bit more cumbersome because you must either hold it in place with your hands or activate your inner thighs. If you attempt to place it between your legs and do not activate the inner thighs, or hold it with your hands, the noodle will pop to the surface of the water due to the buoyant property of water. Of course, activating is not always a negative thing—the more muscles you activate, the more calories you burn. However, you can always choose to use a buoyant belt, which is secured around your waist. You will not have to hold on to the belt if you choose to use it as a buoyant device in the deep water. It is a personal choice, so feel free to experiment with both options.

If you choose a water belt, get accustomed to it in the shallow end before you venture into the deep end. With some body types, the belt causes the hips to rise behind and float out of the water. In this case, reverse the belt by placing the wide part on the front side of your body. Whichever way you wear the belt, make sure that it is tightly secured. If it rides up around your chest as you work your way through the exercises, stop and tighten it so that it remains in position around your waist.

Many people are uncomfortable with deep-water exercises due to fear of the water and being unable to touch the bottom. If this is the case for you, feel free to skip this section. If you are fearful, you will find yourself tensing in the water, your posture will suffer, and you will be more likely to injure yourself. If, on the other hand, you are not a strong swimmer but want to attempt the exercises presented in this chapter, make sure that a lifeguard is present. You might even want to tell him or her that you will be in the deep end and are not a strong swimmer.

If you decide that these exercises can be effective for you, you are in for some great benefits. Exercising in deep water virtually eliminates all of the impact forces on the joints. Because your body is buoyant, you can move your joints through a larger range of motion, which helps increase your flexibility.

In addition, your core muscles are challenged by the task of keeping you upright in the deep water with a flotation device. In fact, when you first enter the deep end, you may feel like a buoy bobbing in the ocean. Your feet may end up in front of or behind you, and the wake of a passing swimmer may tip you over like a rocking horse. The work of counteracting these forces and keeping your body upright with a tight core improves your muscular endurance and posture. Over time, it gets easier to stay upright as you do your exercises.

In mastering most or all of the exercises presented in the preceding chapters, you have increased your cardiovascular endurance and your muscular endurance. As a result, when you start performing the exercises presented in this chapter, you can base your performance on time rather than on number of repetitions. This approach is made easier by the fact that most public pools have a lap clock. Begin by doing each exercise for 30 seconds; if you can maintain proper form for that period without getting winded, try for 45 seconds the next time. Remember that progressive overload means you increase your time gradually. Avoid making large jumps in duration.

One exercise presented at the end of this chapter—the log roll—requires the head to go into the water. As a result, nonswimmers may be uncomfortable with it; if that is the case for you, feel free to skip this exercise. It does provide a great way to strengthen the torso, but those muscles are also activated by exercises presented in chapter 6.

DEEP-WATER FLOTATION JACK 7.1

Equipment

Flotation belt or pool noodle

Exercise Focus

Activates the muscles in the legs and core.

Starting Position

Hang straight down into deep water with either the noodle supporting you or a flotation belt around your waist (a).

Action

1. Scull with your arms and use your outer thighs to pull your legs comfortably apart (b).
2. Continue to scull with your arms and use your inner thighs to return your legs to the starting position (a).

Variation

To increase the activation of your inner and outer thighs, cross your legs when you pull them back into the starting position.

Keep It Safe

Start with small movements if you have minimal range of motion in a hip joint due to injury or surgery.

7.2 DEEP-WATER FLOTATION CROSS-COUNTRY

Equipment

Flotation belt or pool noodle

Exercise Focus

Activates the muscles in the legs and core.

Starting Position

Hang straight down into deep water with either a pool noodle supporting you or a flotation belt around your waist (a).

Action

1. Scull with your arms and open your legs—one to the front and one to the back—as far as is comfortable (b).
2. Once you have opened your legs, reverse their position, keeping them straight as they pass underneath your body (a).

Variation

To use your arm muscles, extend your arms to the front and back in opposition to your legs. If the right leg is extended to the front and the left leg is extended to the back, the left arm should be in front and the right in back.

Keep It Safe

If the straight-leg position stresses your lower back, bend your knees slightly throughout the entire exercise. If you are in rehabilitation after an injury or surgery, start with a small range of motion and increase it gradually.

a

b

DEEP-WATER RUNNING 7.3

Equipment

Flotation belt or pool noodle

Exercise Focus

Activates the muscles in the legs and core.

Starting Position

In deep water, support your body by sitting on a noodle or with a flotation belt around your waist.

Action

1. Mimic the motions of running on land; specifically, pull your knees up to hip level in an alternating fashion and move your arms in opposition to your legs (a).
2. You can lean slightly forward and use the running motion to travel forward (b).

Variation

Once you become proficient with deep-water running in a straight line, add a balance challenge by leaning slightly in one direction or the other to travel in various patterns—for example, a circle, an S, or a figure 8.

Keep It Safe

If pulling your knees all the way to hip level is uncomfortable for your lower back, you can decrease the range of motion.

7.4 DEEP-WATER ROPE JUMP

Equipment

Pool noodle and possibly a flotation belt

Exercise Focus

Activates muscles throughout the body.

Starting Position

Hold the noodle in front of you in a U shape with one hand on each end. Hang your body straight down in the water (a). If you are more comfortable using a flotation belt, attach it securely around your waist.

Action

1. Engage your core, bend your knees, and pull them to your chest as you activate your chest and arm muscles to push the noodle down into the water (b).
2. As your legs come up and your arms push the noodle down, pull your legs through the space between your body and the noodle so that you end up with your feet in front of the noodle (c).
3. Extend your legs forward and perform the exercise in reverse. Specifically, bend your knees, tuck them to your chest as your arms push the noodle down, and bring your legs back over the noodle into the starting position (a).

Variation

As you begin to experiment with this exercise, it is fine if your legs cross over the noodle with one slightly in front of the other. As your core gets stronger, it will become easier to keep your knees together and move your legs as one unit.

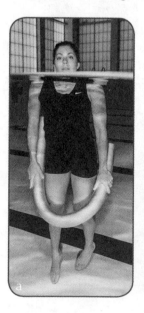

DEEP-WATER WALKING STICK 7.5

Equipment

Flotation belt or pool noodle

Exercise Focus

Activates the muscles in the legs and core.

Starting Position

Hang straight down into deep water with either the noodle supporting you or a flotation belt around your waist (a). Your hands will be sculling in a circular motion to help keep your body in one place

Action

1. Keeping your left leg straight down, directly below your hip joint, engage the muscles in your right hip and upper leg to pull your right leg out in front of you (b).
2. Once your leg is lifted as high as you find comfortable, engage the muscles in the back of your right hip and the back of your right leg to pull your right leg back to the starting position (a). Perform the same motion with your left leg.

Variation

If lifting a straight leg is uncomfortable for your lower back, feel free to slightly bend the leg that you are moving to the front.

Keep It Safe

This should be a slow, controlled exercise. Return your extended leg fully to the starting position before you move the other leg.

7.6 FREE-HANGING LEG CIRCLE

Equipment

Flotation belt or pool noodle

Exercise Focus

Activates the muscles in the hips and core.

Starting Position

Hang straight down into deep water with either the noodle supporting you or a flotation belt around your waist.

Action

1. Scull the water with your arms and keep your legs straight and together and hanging directly underneath your hips.
2. Pretend to trace a small paper plate on the pool bottom with your feet, first moving clockwise and then moving counterclockwise. Move the leg from the hip joint.

Variation

If the muscles in your hips or core are weak (due to injury or surgery, for example), feel free to use only one leg at a time. Pull the mobile leg slightly to the front or side and pretend to trace the plate with your toes but move the leg from the hip joint. Do both sides and circle in both directions.

Keep It Safe

Brace your core so that only your hip joint moves. Anyone sitting near the pool should see your upper body remaining stationary as if you were simply doing a balanced hang.

DEEP-WATER SEATED CORE 7.7

Equipment

Pool noodle or possibly a flotation belt

Exercise Focus

Activates the core, hip, and triceps muscles.

Starting Position

With the noodle or a flotation belt around your waist, extend your legs straight out in front of you (a).

Action

Engaging the muscles in your core and hips and maintaining a right angle at your hip joints, straighten your arms as you push the noodle down into the water and hold it there (b).

Variation

Once you have mastered the hold position, you can make the movement dynamic by repeatedly straightening and bending your elbows.

Keep It Safe

If keeping your legs straight in front of you causes pain in your lower back, bend at the knee joints so that your body position resembles sitting in a straight-backed chair.

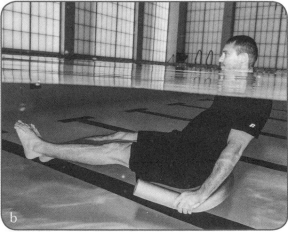

7.8 LOG ROLL

Equipment

Beach ball and possibly a flotation belt

Exercise Focus

Activates the muscles in the core, hips, and legs.

Starting Position

With your stomach toward the pool bottom, extend your body in a straight, horizontal line and look down into the water while holding the beach ball directly under your chest with straight arms (a). Optional: You may choose to wear a flotation belt around your torso.

Action

1. Engaging your core and keeping your legs straight, move in one fluid motion to pull the ball to your chest and roll onto your back, all the while keeping your body in a straight line as if you were a log (b).
2. Reverse in the opposite direction to return to the starting position.

Variation

Until you become comfortable with this move, you may pull your knees into a tuck at the same time that you pull the ball to your chest and roll over. Once you are on your back, straighten your legs and hold that position for three seconds before you reverse.

PART III

EXERCISES FOR COMMON INJURIES AND CONDITIONS

In this section of *Water Exercise*, each chapter addresses a specific area of the body that is susceptible to injury or surgery and may require rehabilitation in the water. As discussed in chapter 1, water exercise is ideal for rehabilitation because of three specific properties of water: buoyancy, hydrostatic pressure, and viscosity. In contrast to the benefits of water exercise, land exercise increases impact on joints due to gravity and ground forces that act on the lower extremities. The pool spares the body from these rigors and therefore provides an excellent place to begin recovery. In fact, some patients find water exercise to be so beneficial that they continue to do it after completing their rehabilitation.

The chapters in this section present therapeutic exercise programs for common injuries in each anatomical region. Each program begins with an entry-level version for people who have just been cleared by their physician for water exercise. The exercise prescriptions include moves from part II of the book, but they may appear here in a different order depending on the relevant injury and the desired rehabilitation.

As you progress through the phases of rehabilitation, remember that recovery comes more quickly for younger people. With this reality in mind, do not become discouraged if your health care provider suggests that you remain in a beginning or intermediate phase of recovery for longer than the suggested period in this book.

Generally, however, after completing a prescribed period (usually two to three weeks) at the beginning level, you can move on to the intermediate level. At this level, the exercises get progressively more difficult and often involve a greater range of motion or slightly more impact. For this reason, you may see exercises for beginning rehabilitation take place in the deep end of the pool.

Deep water can be intimidating for an individual who has not been active, but it is also the one place in the pool where injured joints experience no impact.

It is usually suggested that you remain at the intermediate level for three to six weeks. Afterward, you can move on to the advanced exercises for eight to twelve weeks or until your health care provider releases you from care. At that point, as discussed in chapters 14 and 15, you can create your own aquatic fitness program.

As mentioned in the opening chapters of the book, water exercise provides a fantastic way to exercise or to rehabilitate an injured body part thanks to several unique properties of water. At the same time, for your safety, it is crucial that you remain mindful of the process of thermoregulation as discussed in chapter 1. The human body possesses the ability to thermoregulate, and the water can take on the heat from the body so the water is warmer. This process can be a great pain reliever because warm water increases blood flow, which helps speed the recovery of an injured area by increasing needed components carried in the blood, such as oxygen and white blood cells.

Most public pools keep the water temperature between 78 and 82 degrees Fahrenheit (between about 25 and 28 degrees Celsius), but you may well find a therapeutic pool that maintains a water temperature in the low 90s Fahrenheit (low 30s Celsius). Remember, however, that as your rehabilitation progresses and you begin to perform more advanced exercises, your body will heat up more in response to the increased movement. As a result, a therapeutic pool may get a bit warm.

This section begins by addressing the lower extremities and progresses to the upper body. Each chapter starts with a short discussion of the relevant joint or region and then addresses specific injuries and surgeries. If a given chapter does not pertain to your specific needs, please skip it—or share it with a friend—since you have already been exposed to all of the exercises contained in it.

CHAPTER 8

ANKLE JOINT

In most animals, the weight of the torso is distributed onto four limbs. In humans, of course, our torso weight is distributed onto only two limbs. As a result, the joints in our lower legs experience a good deal of use—and abuse. In particular, the ankle joint not only bears the weight of the body but also contributes to the mobility and stability that we need for everyday locomotor activities, such as walking, jumping over puddles, and running after our children and pets.

These movements require great strength and flexibility, which is why our feet contain more than 20 bones, 20 joints, and 20 muscles. Every day, these body parts are exposed to hundreds of stressors, including high heels, poorly fitted shoes, uneven pavement, hard concrete floors, and perhaps poor posture or poor gait patterns. Therefore, injuries to the foot and ankle account for a large proportion of lower-extremity discomfort.

Of all of the joints in the foot, the ankle joint possesses the greatest range of motion, which is why it is so often injured by a fracture, sprain, or strain. You can greatly reduce your risk of injury, however, if you increase the stability of a joint by strengthening the muscles and ligaments surrounding it. You also then enjoy the benefit of stronger muscles when engaged in various activities, such as propelling yourself forward while walking or even just holding your balance on tiptoe. In addition, because the forces experienced by the ankle joint increase with body weight, rehabilitation for ankle injury should include, where needed, the reduction of body mass. Water exercise is an excellent option due to the elimination of stress on the body's joints due to the water's buoyancy.

COMMON INJURIES
OF THE ANKLE AND FOOT

Common ankle and foot problems include ankle sprain, overuse injuries (plantar fasciitis, Achilles tendinitis, and shin splints), nerve compression, and fracture. Ankle sprain is the most common of all movement-related injuries, especially for people involved in sport or dance activities. A sprain is a traumatic injury of a joint's ligament—a tissue that connects bone to bone. When a sprain occurs, the person often hears a small pop, which is followed immediately by pain, swelling, and a decrease in range of motion. The damage can vary from stretching the ligament to completely tearing the connection.

Ankle sprains can occur on either side of the ankle but usually occur on the outer (lateral) side because it has weaker support than the inner (medial) side. Specifically, the inner side is covered by a thicker membranous capsule than that of the outer side. If you suffer a sprain, your health care provider may X-ray the injured area to rule out a fracture before instructing you to ice the joint and brace or tape it until you are cleared to use it freely. Ligaments can heal, but the rate of healing varies depending on the severity of the injury and the blood supply to the joint. The exercises to increase the blood supply without putting any load on the joint are outlined in chapter 7. These exercises will increase blood flow to the area without putting any stress on the ankle joint at all. As the injury heals and you move into the Intermediate exercises, you can begin putting some load on the joint. As you will see, these exercises include some movements where the foot is placed on the noodle which will activate the muscles surrounding the ankle joint.

Overuse injuries occur when a body part is subjected to excessive demand for a long period of time. The circumstances can vary greatly—for example, training for an athletic event or performing repetitive motions in one's daily work. Overuse injury is often diagnosed when a joint becomes inflamed, and the term for an overuse injury often includes the familiar suffix "itis." Common overuse injuries of the ankle and foot include plantar fasciitis, Achilles tendinitis, and shin splints. Most overuse injuries are treated with a regimen summarized by the acronym PRICE: protect during activity, rest when possible, ice, compress, and elevate when needed.

Plantar fasciitis involves inflammation, and often micro-tearing, of the fascia that runs the entire length of the bottom of the foot. Fascia is connective tissue that forms a web throughout the body to hold structures in place. Because the plantar fascia runs from the heel bone all the way to the toes, plantar fasciitis is extremely painful when walking. It is also the most common cause of heel pain, especially in obese individuals and those who spend long hours on their feet. The goal of rehabilitation in this case is to strengthen and stretch the muscles in the bottom of the foot without overdoing the impact on the heel joint.

Achilles tendinitis is a common injury of the foot and lower leg that usually results from overtraining or overuse. The Achilles tendon runs up the back of the calf, and injuries in this area are common, both among athletes and in the general population, especially older adults. If this overuse condition persists without medical intervention, it can eventually lead to partial or complete tearing of the tendon.

The sharp burning pain associated with this injury is usually worse in the morning, and it increases with activity and can interfere with activities of daily life. It may also be accompanied by swelling and redness. Solutions for alleviating pain and preventing progression of the injury include weight loss and strengthening and stretching programs.

Shin splints is an overuse injury that occurs when repetitive loading of the lower leg causes micro-tearing of the shin muscle. This injury is often accompanied by weak muscles in the lower leg, and other contributors may include lack of flexibility and inability of the lower leg to absorb shock. The condition produces pain and tenderness on the inside (medial) surface of the shin.

Rehabilitation for this injury should begin in the deep end of the pool in order to avoid the stress of impact forces. When you progress to the shallow end, make sure that the water is shallow enough for you to avoid standing on your toes, which would aggravate this injury. Shin splints can be managed through a low-impact exercise program or a stretching and strengthening program that prepares the participant to return to full activities.

Nerve compression, also known as compression neuropathy, can occur anywhere in the body. In the foot, it is most often experienced as tarsal tunnel syndrome, which causes foot numbness radiating to the toes, as well as pain, an electric burning sensation, and a tingling in the foot and heel. It can also cause inflammation and swelling. Inflammation and swelling are two different symptoms and one can be experienced without the other being present in the affected area. Inflammation is a localized response to tissue injury characterized by heat, pain, and redness. Swelling, or edema, is an accumulation of fluid around a joint.

The many possible causes of nerve compression include rheumatoid arthritis, varicose veins, bone spurs, and flat feet. As the pressure increases, the blood flow decreases, and the condition worsens as fluid collects in the foot. Fluid accumulation can be reduced by the hydrostatic pressure experienced by the body in the pool (see chapter 1 for a detailed explanation). It may also be helpful to strengthen the muscles in the shin. If surgery is required, water exercise is a great way to rehabilitate the injured area.

Fractures can occur in many ways, ranging from motor vehicle crashes to sport-related injuries. A stress fracture is a micro break in a bone that is caused by overuse; it can progress into a full break. Any fracture needs to be treated by a doctor, and the patient needs to keep the bone from bearing weight during the recovery.

Following clearance from the physician, the person can begin gradually returning to weight-bearing activity in the pool as his or her range of motion increases. The deep end of the pool is the perfect place to start by simply mimicking the basic movements of walking. The exerciser can then progress to lateral work and eventually to exercising in the shallow end.

EXERCISES FOR ANKLE AND FOOT REHABILITATION

The activities presented in the following tables are ordered by the chapter in which they are described. For instance, to keep the ankle free of impact, exercises performed in deep water would be best for a beginner, and these exercises are presented at the top of each table. Glancing down through the table reveals that the intermediate and advanced exercises are pulled from the chapters that address exercising in the shallow end. The intermediate exercises do not involve any rebounding; in fact, these exercises can often be done while grounded on the bottom of the pool. The advanced exercises do involve a rebound or bounce, and they are appropriate as your joint returns to normal and your rehabilitation process comes to a close.

Table 8.1 lists relevant exercises that you are familiar with from chapters 3 through 7. The beginning exercises are performed in deep water, which protects the joint from impact. This work increases the range of motion around the joint without threat of additional injury. As your recovery progresses, you can move on to the intermediate exercises, which include suspended, neutral, and grounded (anchored) moves in the shallow end of the pool. The shallow end provides a buoyant atmosphere that allows you to put some weight on the injured area without subjecting it to any rebounding impact.

After completing the intermediate exercises without pain or increased tenderness, you can progress to the advanced exercises, which allow you to put weight on the joint while also increasing its range of motion. Use caution when you first begin to put weight on the joint. As your rehabilitation progresses, the joint will be able to withstand more pressure, and eventually you will be injury free.

Table 8.1 Exercises for Ankle and Foot Rehabilitation

Ankle exercises		Sets and reps or duration
Beginning exercises		
7.1 Deep-water flotation jack (p. 123)		2 or 3 sets of 12 reps
7.2 Deep-water flotation cross-country (p. 124)		2 or 3 sets of 12 reps
7.3 Deep-water running (p. 125)		2 or 3 sets of 3 minutes
7.5 Deep-water walking stick (p. 127)		2 or 3 sets of 12 reps
7.6 Free-hanging leg circle (p. 128)		2 or 3 sets of one minute in each direction

(continued)

TABLE 8.1   Exercises for Ankle and Foot Rehabilitation *(continued)*

Ankle exercises	Sets and reps or duration
Intermediate exercises	
6.7 Suspended jack (p. 104)	3 or 4 sets of 12 reps
6.8 Suspended eggbeater (p. 105)	3 or 4 sets of one minute
6.13 Noodle balance (p. 112)	3 or 4 sets of one minute
5.13 Neutral jack (p. 77)	3 or 4 sets of 12 reps
5.14 Neutral cross-country (p. 78)	3 or 4 sets of 12 reps

Ankle exercises		Sets and reps or duration
Intermediate exercises *(continued)*		
5.25 Single-leg press (p. 90)		2 or 3 sets of 12 reps
Flexibility: standing calf stretch (chapter 3) (p. 34)		2 or 3 sets of 30 seconds
4.5 Calf raise (p. 43)		2 or 3 sets of 12 reps
4.6 Squat (p. 44)		2 or 3 sets of 12 reps
Advanced exercises		
6.9 Double-leg push-down (p. 106)		3 or 4 sets of one minute

(continued)

TABLE 8.1 Exercises for Ankle and Foot Rehabilitation *(continued)*

Ankle exercises		Sets and reps or duration
Advanced exercises *(continued)*		
6.17 Side-balance lean (p. 116)		3 or 4 sets of one minute
5.16 Carioca (p. 80)		3 or 4 sets of one minute
5.17 Serpentine running (p. 82)		3 or 4 sets of one minute
5.20 Side squat (p. 85)		3 or 4 sets of 12 reps
5.21 Walking lunge (p. 86)		3 or 4 sets of 12 reps

Ankle exercises		Sets and reps or duration
Advanced exercises *(continued)*		
5.22 Straight-leg zombie walk (p. 87)		3 or 4 sets of 12 reps
5.23 Tightrope traveling (p. 88)		3 or 4 sets of 12 reps

CHAPTER 9

KNEE JOINT

The knee joint, which connects the thigh bone to the larger of the two lower leg bones, is a hinge point (with a slight bit of rotation) that is capable of flexion and extension, or bending and straightening. The weight-bearing knee is subjected to great stress from both above and below. Specifically, it is constantly pushed down on by body mass and gravity, and it also experiences impact forces coming up from below. Indeed, as we live our daily lives—running, climbing stairs, wearing ill-fitting shoes, and so on—our activities can wreak havoc on our knee joints.

It is not surprising, then, that the knee joint is vulnerable and frequently injured. The injuries often relate to poor conditioning, overtraining, lower-body alignment problems, or improper gait. Gait issues manifest in walking patterns when a person is, for example, knock-kneed, bowlegged, or flat-footed. All of these conditions affect the way in which the muscles in the lower leg pull on the knee joint.

Of course, knee injuries can also result from sport participation and other vigorous activities. Traumatic injury often involves the many ligaments that cross the knee when they are subjected to twisting action, high friction, or movement on an uneven surface. For example, athletes who make sudden turns or stops are extremely vulnerable to tearing the ligaments in the knee joint. Members of the general population can experience the same tears just from walking on an uneven surface or from any application of force that causes a twisting action in the knee. Simply put, any quick turn on a weight-bearing knee leaves the joint vulnerable to a ligamentous injury.

Most overuse injuries of the knee involve anterior knee pain, or pain in the front of the knee. More specifically, pain in the patella (kneecap) can be associated with tight hamstrings, tight quadriceps, or changes in gait due to pregnancy or weight gain. Other patellar pain syndromes are associated with cartilage destruction or a dislocated patella, which is a vital part of the joint because it increases the leverage of the knee. The knee joint is a large synovial joint—meaning that it contains a joint-lubricating fluid secreted by a synovial membrane—so one of the first symptoms of patellar discomfort is swelling. When the knee joint becomes injured or inflamed due to overuse, the synovial membrane secretes more fluid as self-protection to prevent more damage. As we age, we make less synovial fluid, which increases the risk of joint discomfort in people over the age of 30.

One important goal of knee rehabilitation is to strengthen the muscles that cross the joint. These muscles, as well as the tendons, provide support to the lower extremity. After rehabilitation, it is important to maintain this strength in order to maintain the integrity of the joint, increase its stability and mobility, and prevent injury.

COMMON INJURIES OF THE KNEE

Common issues in this area of the body include patellar (kneecap) conditions, infrapatellar tendinitis ("jumper's knee"), ligament injury, torn meniscus, osteo-arthritis, and knee joint replacement. Patellar conditions, also known as patel-lofemoral pain syndrome, consist mainly of overuse syndromes associated with overloading the knee or subjecting it to repeated trauma. In such cases, symptoms can often be reduced simply by changing the activity or mode of exercise. Other possible causes include improper footwear and postsurgical complications.

Patellar conditions include chondromalacia, patellar bursitis, and patellar subluxation. Because these conditions are similar to each other, the appropriate exercise guidelines can be generalized. The most important consideration in rehabbing the anterior knee is to limit the amount of flexion in the joint. There-fore, the recommended exercises are structured to emphasize the straightening of the knee as opposed to any deep bending.

Chondromalacia, often referred to as "runner's knee," occurs most often in active young adults. It affects the cartilage on the movable surface of the knee-cap. Most often, it involves softening or degeneration of the cartilage between the patella and the head of the femur (thigh bone). Common symptoms include swelling, a grating sensation, and pain during movement.

Patellar bursitis is sometimes referred to as "housemaid's knee" because it is seen most often in people who kneel for extended periods of time—for example, housekeepers, tile or brick layers, landscapers, and gardeners. In these cases, bursitis results from prolonged or excessive pressure on the joint. It can also result from traumatic injury or an inflammatory condition, such as rheumatoid arthritis.

Patellar subluxation, also referred to as an unstable kneecap, simply means that the patella does not move evenly within the groove of the femur. Some people call it patellofemoral malalignment because the two bony structures do not line up properly in the joint.

Infrapatellar tendinitis is a chronic syndrome that often affects individuals who participate in jumping activities, such as basketball and volleyball. The jumping motion causes stress in the tendons of the knee. The condition can also be caused by improper training conditions, muscle imbalance, and lack of flexibility. The inflammation occurs in the tendon connecting the kneecap to the tibia, the larger bone of the lower leg. As a result, pain from this injury is reported most often in the portion of the kneecap that is closer to the tibia. Rehabilitation for this injury includes strengthening and stretching of the lower extremity.

Ligament injuries of the knee are increasing in number, especially among women. Ligaments are most often torn when running and making a quick cut to change direction or making a quick stop. The most common site of ligament injury in the knee is the anterior cruciate ligament. This injury often results in difficulty with rotational or side-to-side movements of the knee joint; it also decreases the range of motion when bending and straightening the knee joint while walking. More generally, however, any ligament tear greatly reduces the stability of the knee joint, and these injuries can occur not only during sport participation but also during normal activities and in motor vehicle accidents. Most full ligament tears require surgery followed by a cycling or aquatic plan of rehabilitation overseen by a physical therapist.

A torn meniscus can result from a torn ligament, because the meniscus connects to certain ligaments in the knee. The meniscus is a C-shaped disc inside the knee joint that is made of fibrocartilage, which is slightly mobile and aids in spreading synovial fluid during knee movement. A torn or partially torn meniscus is a common knee injury that often causes pain and intermittent bouts of locking or buckling in the knee joint. In addition, a torn meniscus often slips away from its proper location, thus hindering the joint's proper mechanical functioning.

Arthritis is a disease that causes inflammation in the joints and surrounding tissue. The most common form of arthritis is osteoarthritis; in fact, by the age of 55, most people have some form of it in at least one joint. Osteoarthritis is not just one condition but a group of disorders in which the protective cartilage over a joint thins or becomes damaged. As a result, the bones rub together, which causes pain, swelling, stiffness, and tenderness around the joint. One of the most commonly affected joints is the knee, and osteoarthritic pain in the knee can be severe enough to alter a person's gait and affect his or her balance. Even so, patients with osteoarthritis are encouraged to engage in some form of activity because the reduction or absence of movement decreases the body's production of synovial fluid, thus increasing the symptoms.

Knee joint replacements are becoming more common every year. The majority are done to increase mobility and overall quality of life. More people are opting for joint replacement in part because of improvements in both the quality of artificial joints and the techniques for implanting them. After the surgery, physicians generally recommend that the patient engage in a reasonable amount of physical activity, which at first is performed under the care of a physical therapist. Specifically, patients are advised to engage in exercise that combines periodization of activity with low-impact forces. Periodization is the process of varying a fitness program at regular time intervals to bring optimal gains in physical performance. These variations may include changing the number of sets and repetitions, varying the length of the rest periods, changing the order of the exercises or introducing new exercises.

EXERCISES FOR KNEE REHABILITATION

The activities presented in the following tables are ordered by the chapter in which they are described. For instance, to keep the knee free of impact, exercises performed in deep water would be best for a beginner, and these exercises are presented at the top of each table. Glancing down through the table reveals that the intermediate and advanced exercises are pulled from the chapters that address exercising in the shallow end. The intermediate exercises do not involve any rebounding; in fact, these exercises can often be done while grounded on the bottom of the pool. The advanced exercises do involve a rebound or bounce, and they are appropriate as your joint returns to normal and your rehabilitation process comes to a close.

Table 9.1 Exercises for Knee Ligament Injuries

Knee joint exercises		Sets and reps or duration
Beginning exercises		
7.3 Deep-water running (p. 125)		2 or 3 sets of 3 minutes
7.4 Deep-water rope jump (p. 126)		2 or 3 sets of 3 minutes
6.7 Suspended jack (p. 104)		2 or 3 sets of 30 seconds
6.8 Suspended eggbeater (p. 105)		2 or 3 sets of 30 seconds
6.10 Side shoot-through (p. 107)		2 or 3 sets of 12 reps

(continued)

TABLE 9.1 Exercises for Knee Ligament Injuries *(continued)*

Knee joint exercises	Sets and reps or duration
Beginning exercises *(continued)*	
6.11 Front and back shoot-through (p. 108) 	2 or 3 sets of 12 reps
6.12 Flotation extension and abduction-adduction (p. 110) 	2 or 3 sets of 12 reps
Intermediate exercises	
6.17 Side-balance lean (p. 116) 	3 or 4 sets of 30 seconds
5.14 Neutral cross-country (p. 78) 	3 or 4 sets of 12 reps
5.25 Single-leg press (p. 90) 	3 or 4 sets of 12 reps

Knee joint exercises		Sets and reps or duration
Intermediate exercises *(continued)*		
4.1 Knee flexion and extension (p. 39)		3 or 4 sets of 12 reps
4.6 Squat (p. 44)		3 or 4 sets of 12 reps
Flexibility—standing quadriceps stretch (chapter 3) (p. 34)		3 or 4 sets of 30 seconds
Advanced exercises		
6.9 Double-leg push-down (p. 106)		3 or 4 sets of 12 reps
5.2 Rocking horse (p. 64)		3 or 4 sets of 12 reps (both sides)

(continued)

TABLE 9.1 Exercises for Knee Ligament Injuries *(continued)*

Knee joint exercises		Sets and reps or duration
Advanced exercises *(continued)*		
5.3 Side mogul (p. 65)		3 or 4 sets of 12 reps
5.6 Soccer kick (p. 68)		3 or 4 sets of 12 reps (both sides)
5.7 Hoedown kick (p. 69)		3 or 4 sets of 12 reps (both sides)
5.11 Tuck jump (p. 75)		3 or 4 sets of 12 reps
5.12 Front-to-back mogul (p. 76)		3 or 4 sets of 12 reps

Knee joint exercises		Sets and reps or duration
Advanced exercises *(continued)*		
5.16 Carioca (p. 80)		3 or 4 sets of 3 minutes
5.20 Side squat (p. 85)		3 or 4 sets of 12 reps
5.21 Walking lunge (p. 86)		3 or 4 sets of 12 reps
Warm-up: dynamic knee lift (chapter 3) (p. 31)		3 or 4 sets of 12 reps

Table 9.2   Exercises for Patellar Injuries

Knee joint exercises	Sets and reps or duration
Beginning exercises	
7.1 Deep-water flotation jack (p. 123)	2 or 3 sets of 12 reps
7.2 Deep-water flotation cross-country (p. 124)	2 or 3 sets of 12 reps
7.5 Deep-water walking stick (p. 127)	2 or 3 sets of 12 reps
7.6 Free-hanging leg circle (p. 128)	2 or 3 sets of 12 reps
6.17 Side-balance lean (p. 116)	2 or 3 sets of 30 seconds

Knee joint exercises	Sets and reps or duration
Beginning exercises	
5.30 Prone hip abduction and adduction (p. 95)	2 or 3 sets of 12 reps
Intermediate exercises	
4.1 Knee flexion and extension (p. 39)	3 or 4 sets of 12 reps
4.2 Hip flexion (p. 40)	3 or 4 sets of 12 reps
4.3 Hip extension (p. 41)	3 or 4 sets of 12 reps

(continued)

Table 9.2 Exercises for Patellar Injuries *(continued)*

Knee joint exercises		Sets and reps or duration
Advanced exercises		
5.1 Straight-leg kick to the front (p. 63)		3 or 4 sets of 12 reps
5.10 Star jack (p. 74)		3 or 4 sets of 12 reps
4.4 Leg swing (p. 42)		3 or 4 sets of 12 reps

CHAPTER 10

HIP JOINT

Hip pain and injury are common among all ages and among both active and sedentary people. The hip is a complex ball-and-socket joint located between the pelvis and the femur. It is surrounded by strong ligaments and 28 thick muscles, which increase the joint's stability and help it withstand repeated motions and a fair amount of wear and tear. This stability is essential for standing, walking, and running.

Because the hip is a ball-and-socket joint, it has a fairly large and fluid range of motion—except when it is restricted by surrounding structures, such as the lower spine. Hip function can be affected by the mechanics of the knee, foot, and ankle. A relatively low incidence of hip injuries occurs among athletes. More generally, however, it is common for a fall to cause a hip fracture; this is especially true as we age and our bones become more brittle.

The hip joint supports the weight of the torso and plays an integral role in the body's stability and mobility. The motions of the hip joint and the lower spine bring about changes in the position of the pelvis and torso. The hip joint and the pelvic girdle also play important roles in maintaining balance and proper posture while standing; therefore, balance enhancement exercises are vital to recovery.

The hip is a relatively stable joint due to the fact that gravity continuously pushes the pelvic girdle down when a person is standing. In addition, the hip joint is attached to the largest muscle in the body—the gluteus maximus—which can generate a great deal of strength while contracted. To guarantee that the posterior gluteus maximus does not overpower the other hip muscles, an exercise program must focus on the anterior muscles as well. These muscles also receive some conditioning during everyday activities, such as walking, rising from or lowering into a chair, and climbing stairs.

The hip joint is designed to withstand a great deal of use, including repeated motion and wear and tear. It is the largest joint in the body, is well adapted to weight-bearing activity, and is designed with a cushion of cartilage that helps prevent excessive friction as the bone moves in the socket. However, this cartilage can wear down and become damaged, which causes discomfort. Muscles and tendons are also subject to overuse injuries.

Depending on which condition causes the hip pain, you may feel discomfort in any region of the hip joint, the groin, or the buttocks. Initial treatment should follow the PRICE acronym: protect during activity, rest when possible, ice, compress, and elevate when needed. In addition, try taking a short time off from the activity to see if the pain eases. If it does, you can begin a slow return to activity in the water under the direction of your health care team. If the pain doesn't ease, you should see your health care provider and follow his or her prescription for either rest or rehabilitation.

COMMON INJURIES OF THE HIP

Common hip conditions include greater trochanter bursitis, iliotibial band syndrome, stress fracture, hip flexor strain, femoral acetabular impingement, piriformis syndrome, hip replacement, arthritis, snapping hip syndrome, and osteonecrosis. Greater trochanter bursitis is a common inflammation of a bursa sac located between the upper leg bone and the posterior hip. It often results in pain and tingling in the affected area. This condition is more common among dancers, cross-country skiers, and runners, but it can also result from trauma due to a fall or a sharp increase in activity. Rehabilitation should focus on regaining flexibility and strength in the hip.

Iliotibial band syndrome is an overuse condition that occurs when a portion of the iliotibial band rubs against the top of the femur. It is common in active individuals of all ages and is caused primarily by improper training, improper footwear, muscle imbalance, and changes in running surfaces. Patients often complain of tightness, burning, or stabbing pain at the outside of the knee and often running up the outside of the thigh. Even though the syndrome causes pain at the knee joint, it is often worsened by weakness in the hip abductors—the muscles that move the leg away from the midline of the body. Therefore, in addition to increasing flexibility, rehabilitation should include exercises that help the patient regain strength at the hip and lateral thigh.

Like the ankle and knee, the hip can also be the site of stress fractures. A stress fracture occurs when a bone cannot accommodate the forces applied to it or when the bone is weak from poor nutrition or insufficient density. Stress fractures manifest in the form of pain that is located on the front of the thigh and travels to the pelvis, back, or any region of the leg. Because stress fractures can progress to full-blown fractures, a physician should X-ray the area before diagnosing the injury. Hip fractures are more common among elderly patients with osteoporosis.

Hip flexor strains involve the muscles that connect the hip to the upper leg. The multiple hip flexors lift the leg when a person walks or runs. A strain is a tear in the muscle, and it causes a stabbing feeling near the hip–leg connection; it will be especially painful when you lie down and pull your knee to your chest. As you begin to rehabilitate after this type of injury, stretching is imperative.

Femoral acetabular impingement occurs when the ball and socket of the hip joint do not match correctly. Instead, the ill-fitting ball grinds and tears the cartilage lining the socket. This injury manifests as a nagging ache in the front of the hip. Recovering from it requires the expertise of a physical therapist for up to eight weeks, and the therapy usually involves water fitness.

Piriformis syndrome involves the piriformis muscle, which sits deep in the hip. If this muscle is tight, it rubs against the sciatic nerve, which causes sharp pain in the buttocks or radiating pain down the back or leg. Once the pain lessens, the risk of reinjury can be reduced by regular stretching.

Hip replacement is one of the most common types of prosthesis-related surgery, and it is often performed to address an arthritic or damaged joint. Hip replacement involves two substitutions: (1) the damaged ball end of the femur is replaced by a metal ball attached to a metal pin and fitted into the thigh bone, and (2) the damaged socket is replaced by a plastic socket in the pelvis. These new materials allow the joint to move normally and without pain.

Exercise is an important part of the rehabilitation process and must be discussed with your physician and physical therapist. This phase of recovery is crucial because the muscles surrounding the hip joint become weak from inactivity. In addition, the joint has a small range of motion following the surgery, but the range generally improves; the extent of this improvement may depend on how stiff the joint was before surgery.

One of the most frequent causes of hip pain is arthritis, which results in inflammation of the hip joint. The arthritis may fall into the category of osteoarthritis (a degenerative joint condition) or of rheumatoid arthritis (a multijoint inflammatory condition seen most often in women). The cartilage affected by arthritis is avascular, meaning that it does not receive a constant flow of blood and nutrients from the heart. For this reason, its healing ability is not good. The body's compensatory system steps in and works for a short period, but this adaptation becomes deficient as a person ages.

Clients with any type of arthritis can benefit from aquatic exercise. The activity needs to remain less intense if the participant is having an arthritis flare-up. The Arthritis Foundation recommends a warm-water pool and has designed a class specifically for participants with arthritis. Instructors who lead this type of class undergo specialized training and certification.

Snapping hip syndrome encompasses three distinct issues in the hip: (1) the iliotibial band snapping over the outside of the thigh, (2) the deep hip flexor snapping over the front of the hip joint, and (3) the labrum causing a snapping sensation. The labrum is the cartilage surrounding the hip joint. When it tears even a tiny bit, it can cause a catching sensation in the hip.

Osteonecrosis occurs when blood flow to an area of bone is restricted. When sufficient blood does not reach a bone, the cells die and the bone begins to collapse. This condition occurs most commonly in the hip. It may be caused by a hip fracture or dislocation.

EXERCISES FOR HIP REHABILITATION

The activities presented in the following table are ordered by the chapter in which they are described. Before you begin the rehabilitation of a hip, check with your health care provider or physical therapist. This is especially important if you have undergone a hip replacement, because each type of replacement requires a slightly different range of motion when beginning rehabilitation.

The first step in any hip rehabilitation is to increase the range of motion while remaining pain free. Exercises for this purpose are performed in deep water using a flotation device. Once your therapist clears you to put some weight on the affected leg, you can progress to the intermediate exercises, which are performed in the shallow end of the pool. During this phase, some therapists may require that you continue using a flotation device to limit the impact now that your feet are touching the bottom of the pool. As your strength and range of motion improve, you will return to performing the exercises that are common to a general fitness routine.

Table 10.1   Exercises for Hip Rehabilitation

Hip exercises	Sets and reps or duration
Beginning exercises	
7.1 Deep-water flotation jack (p. 123)	2 or 3 sets of 12
7.2 Deep-water flotation cross-country (p. 124)	2 or 3 sets of 12
7.3 Deep-water running (p. 125)	2 or 3 sets of 3 minutes
7.4 Deep-water rope jump (p. 126)	2 or 3 sets of 12 reps
7.5 Deep-water walking stick (p. 127)	2 or 3 sets of 12 reps

(continued)

Table 10.1 Exercises for Hip Rehabilitation *(continued)*

Hip exercises	Sets and reps or duration
Beginning exercises *(continued)*	
7.6 Free-hanging leg circles (p. 128) 	2 or 3 sets of 12 reps
6.12 Flotation extension and abduction-adduction (p. 110) 	2 or 3 sets of 12 reps
4.2 Hip flexion (p. 40) 	3 or 4 sets of 12 reps
4.3 Hip extension (p. 41) 	3 or 4 sets of 12 reps
Intermediate exercises	
6.17 Side-balance lean (p. 116) 	3 or 4 sets of 30 seconds

Hip exercises	Sets and reps or duration
Intermediate exercises _(continued)_	
5.20 Side squat (p. 85)	3 or 4 sets of 12 reps
5.21 Walking lunge (p. 86)	3 or 4 sets of 12 reps
5.22 Straight-leg zombie walk (p. 87)	3 or 4 sets of 12 reps
5.30 Prone hip abduction and adduction (p. 95)	3 or 4 sets of 12 reps
4.4 Leg swing (p. 42)	3 or 4 sets of 12 reps

(continued)

Table 10.1 Exercises for Hip Rehabilitation *(continued)*

Hip exercises		Sets and reps or duration
Intermediate exercises *(continued)*		
4.7 Hip abduction and adduction (p. 45)		3 or 4 sets of 12 reps
4.8 Jumping jacks (p. 46)		3 or 4 sets of 12 reps
Advanced exercises		
6.6 Rebounding leg swing (p. 103)		3 or 4 sets of 12 reps
5.1 Straight-leg kick to the front (p. 63)		3 or 4 sets of 12 reps
5.5 Pendulum (p. 67)		3 or 4 sets of 12 reps

Hip exercises		Sets and reps or duration
Advanced exercises (*continued*)		
5.8 Rear kick (p. 70)		3 or 4 sets of 12 reps
5.9 Criss-cross jumping jack (p. 72)		3 or 4 sets of 12 reps
5.10 Star jack (p. 74)		3 or 4 sets of 12 reps
5.23 Tightrope traveling (p. 88)		3 or 4 sets of 12 reps
5.30 Prone hip abduction and adduction (p. 95)		3 or 4 sets of 12 reps

CHAPTER II

SPINE

The spine is a column or tower of 33 small bones that supports the head and upper body. The small bones, or vertebrae, interlock in a series of joints that glide or slide. This gliding motion is what gives the backbone its flexibility. Each vertebra contains a region specifically made to bear weight, and the area between vertebrae contains cartilage with a jelly-like middle that acts as a shock absorber. During improper movements, this jelly-like substance can seep through the cartilage and cause further damage and pain. Therefore, it is crucial that we use the spinal column with proper care and alignment.

The spine or backbone fulfills multiple key functions. For one thing, it can bend and rotate in many directions. It also protects the spinal cord, which in turn protects the nerves involved in sensory input and muscle movement. For this reason, the spine must remain properly aligned and stable during all forms of movement and stress. The mobility of the spine is extremely complex—more so than that of any other joint we have discussed. Motion in the spinal cord itself is minimal between the vertebrae or discs; the spine as a whole, however, is capable of a tremendous amount of movement.

The spinal column is composed of four main segments: cervical, thoracic, lumbar, and sacral. At each transition from one segment to another, you would find a slight curve in the spine if you could see it from the side. In some individuals, these curves are exaggerated, which can lead to back pain or problems in movement patterns.

Even with normal curvature of the spine, the torso is subjected to tremendous forces. We must deal not only with the ever-present force of gravity but also with constant intra-abdominal pressure, tension in attached ligaments and surrounding muscles, and the external loads that we frequently place on the spine—for example, book bags, purses, and luggage. It is no wonder, then, that more than 80 percent of the American population suffers from back pain at some point in life. Indeed, back pain is one of the most common reasons that people visit orthopedic specialists.

The connective tissue structures in your back—your tendons and ligaments—adapt to the position in which they are held on a daily basis. Think, for example, of poor sitting positions during long commutes, poor working conditions in front of the computer, and just plain poor posture. Spending extended time in such positions can cause rounding of the upper back or reduce the lordotic curve in the lower back. Everyone has a small lordotic curve in the lumbar, or lower portion of the back. This is one of three normal curvatures in the spinal column. When the curve is extreme, it is called lordosis. Some individuals will experience lordosis from participation in athletic events such as gymnastics or diving. These athletes may not experience pain because of the strength of the muscles in the core. Others may experience pain. The bottom line is that proper posture creates a strong core, and a strong core supports proper posture.

Fortunately, the potential damage from everyday sitting and standing positions can be minimized by maintaining proper posture with the shoulders retracted and pulled down and the chest lifted. We refer to this proper posture as having a "neutral spine," which can be defined simply as the absence of tension in the neck and low lumbar region. This posture helps us maintain the normal curves that are necessary for a strong and properly aligned spine.

The most commonly injured part of the back is the lower lumbar region. This region contains the strongest and largest vertebrae, but these injuries usually take the form of a soft-tissue injury to either a ligament (sprain) or a muscle (strain). Although the pain originates in the back, it may eventually radiate into the hip, which often makes diagnosis difficult. Other common back injuries include minor fractures, which usually result from a blow or other traumatic event and are often found in the cervical and sacral regions. However, back injuries can also occur anywhere along the vertebral column due to sport participation and activities of everyday living.

Without activity the spinal structure becomes deconditioned. In this case, the muscles can no longer support the back properly, and injury becomes more likely. For this reason, exercise is prescribed more often than bed rest. Movement also helps exchange nutrients and fluids within the spinal discs.

Conditions of the spine often lead to low-back pain, which can be accompanied by loss of motion, loss of strength, and reduced function. Exercise is often prescribed, and it tends to include some common guidelines.

- If the exercise causes an increase in pain, decrease the range of motion or avoid the exercise altogether.
- Practice bracing your abdominals (as if someone were going to punch you in the stomach) to protect your lumbar spine. Bracing is preferable to "sucking in" or "hollowing out" the abdominal region.
- Constantly emphasize good posture, which means aligning your ears, shoulders, and hips.
- Stretch your torso and lower extremities to increase your range of motion. Tight hamstrings (in the upper back of the leg) are the number one cause of low-back pain.

COMMON INJURIES OF THE SPINE

Common spinal injuries include herniation of a lumbar or cervical disc, lumbar or cervical spinal stenosis, spondylolisthesis, sciatica, osteoporosis, and cervical radiculopathy. A herniated lumbar or cervical disc is also known as a ruptured disc. In many cases, this injury is initiated during a routine weightlifting event or a quick turn or pivot in everyday life. Whatever the precipitating event, the injury is caused by displacement of a disc's center through a crack in the outer layer. The displacement invades the space where nerves run through the spinal cord.

The pressure from the herniated disc may cause pain in the back, as well as pain, tingling, and numbness in the legs, shoulders, and arms. If the disc is located in the upper cervical region of the neck, the injury will affect the upper extremities. If the disc is located in the lower back or lumbar region, the injury will affect the legs. Exercises that cause rotation of the spine should be avoided by people with this injury, especially in the seated position.

Lumbar or cervical spinal stenosis involves a narrowing of the spinal canal, which compresses the nerves in the spinal cord. Spinal stenosis often produces no signs or symptoms; however, it can cause pain, tingling, or numbness in the legs if it is lumbar-related or in the upper extremities if it is cervical. It can also cause weakness in the affected limbs. Exercises that involve extreme flexion, or bending backward, should be avoided by people with this injury.

Spondylolisthesis is an acquired malformation of the spinal column that usually results from extensive and repetitive hyperextension of the lumbar spine. It is a degenerative disc disease in which bone underlying the cartilage is rubbed ragged. The damaged projections can cause stiffness, muscles spasm, and restriction of movement. This injury is often seen in athletes who spend a large amount of time with the back arched—for example, gymnasts, football players, and divers. Older adults may experience a stress fracture in a vertebra or a crack that does not heal. Such an injury may not cause any issues at all, but it is possible for the injured vertebra to slip over another. When slippage occurs, the injured vertebrae may no longer be connected to the one below, causing support of the spinal column to be compromised.

Sciatica occurs when a disc slips slightly and presses down on a spinal nerve root. The sciatic nerve is a large nerve starting in the low back and extending down the back of the leg. As a result, sciatica causes acute pain to radiate down the back of the leg and often into the foot. The pain varies from infrequent and irritating to severe and debilitating. It can be worsened by spondylolisthesis, obesity, inactivity, and pregnancy.

Osteoporosis is the most common bone disease in developed countries. It is a condition of low bone mass that can cause deterioration of bone structure anywhere in the body, and one of the most common locations for it is the spine. The deterioration increases the risk of fracture in the diseased bone even without any major trauma. As a result, a fracture can be caused even by an everyday activity, such as carrying a package or getting in or out of a car. The risk of osteoporosis is increased by certain genetic factors, obesity, prior injuries, and persistent wear and tear.

Cervical radiculopathy involves a loss of upper extremity function as the result of irritation or compression of a spinal nerve root in the neck. It disturbs nerve function and can cause pain and loss of sensation in the upper extremities.

Symptoms may include muscle weakness, lack of coordination, and a tingling in the hands or fingers. Gentle mobilization during exercise often helps decrease the pain.

EXERCISES FOR SPINE REHABILITATION

The two most important factors in spine rehabilitation are the stability and mobility of the spine. Both factors can be improved by any exercise that strengthens the muscles, ligaments, and tendons surrounding the spine. To maximize these two factors while remaining pain free, some of the exercises listed in table 11.1 begin in the neutral or grounded position to avoid unnecessary jarring of the spinal cord. The table also includes beginning exercises, performed with a flotation device, that emphasize the stability of the spine while you move another body part. As you work through both of these types of exercises, remember to start with a small range of motion and progress slowly. As your rehabilitation continues, you will be able to move through larger movement patterns as your stability and mobility increase.

The exercises in this chapter are designed to be completed in the order listed in the chart. The initial exercises of each section will activate the muscles surrounding the spinal cord. The beginning exercises begin with a trunk rotation so that the spine is prepared for any rotation that may occur in the noodle bicycle riding. In the intermediate and advanced sections, the planks will activate the muscles so they are prepared for exercises that require the bracing of the muscles surrounding the spine.

Table 11.1 Exercises for Spine Rehabilitation

Spine exercises		Sets and reps or duration
Beginning exercises		
4.11 Trunk rotation (p. 52)		2 or 3 sets of 12–15 reps
4.14 Noodle bicycle riding (p. 56)		2 or 3 sets of 3 minutes
5.24 Lateral trunk flexion (p. 89)		2 or 3 sets of 12–15 reps
6.13 Noodle balance (p. 112)		2 or 3 sets of 1 minute
7.1 Deep-water flotation jack (p. 123)		2 or 3 sets of 12–15 reps

(continued)

Table 11.1 Exercises for Spine Rehabilitation *(continued)*

Spine exercises	Sets and reps or duration
Beginning exercises *(continued)*	
7.2 Deep-water flotation cross-country (p. 124)	2 or 3 sets of 12–15 reps
Warm-up: chest opener (chapter 3) (p. 30)	2 or 3 sets of 1 minute
Flexibility: standing side stretch (chapter 3) (p. 35)	2 or 3 sets of 1 minute
Flexibility: standing hip stretch (chapter 3) (p. 35)	2 or 3 sets of 1 minute
Intermediate exercises	
6.14 Stationary plank (p. 113) 	2 or 3 sets of 1 minute

Spine exercises		Sets and reps or duration
Intermediate exercises *(continued)*		
6.17 Side-balance lean (p. 116)		2 or 3 sets of 1 minute
7.3 Deep-water running (p. 125)		2 or 3 sets of 1 minute
7.6 Free-hanging leg circle (p. 128)		2 or 3 sets of 1 minute
7.7 Deep-water seated core (p. 129)		2 or 3 sets of 12–15 reps
Warm-up: chest opener (chapter 3) (p. 30)		3 or 4 sets of 1 minute

(continued)

Table 11.1 Exercises for Spine Rehabilitation *(continued)*

Spine exercises	Sets and reps or duration
Intermediate exercises *(continued)*	
Flexibility: standing side stretch (chapter 3) (p. 35) 	3 or 4 sets of 1 minute
Flexibility: standing hip stretch (chapter 3) (p. 35) 	3 or 4 sets of 1 minute
Advanced exercises	
6.15 Side noodle plank (p. 114) 	2 or 3 sets of 1 minute
6.16 Plank sculling (p. 115) 	2 or 3 sets of 1 minute
6.20 Wood chop (p. 119) 	2 or 3 sets of 12–15 reps

Spine exercises	Sets and reps or duration
Advanced exercises *(continued)*	
7.8 Log roll (p. 130) 	2 or 3 sets of 12–15 reps
Warm-up: chest opener (chapter 3) (p. 30) 	3 or 4 sets of 1 minute
Flexibility: standing side stretch (chapter 3) (p. 35) 	3 or 4 sets of 1 minute
Flexibility: standing hip stretch (chapter 3) (p. 35) 	3 or 4 sets of 1 minute

CHAPTER 12

SHOULDER JOINT

The shoulder is the most complex joint structure in the human body because it contains multiple articulations or joints. The more articulations a structure includes, the more movement it can produce, and what we generally refer to as the (single) shoulder joint actually includes five articulations, which makes it the most movable joint in the body.

The shoulder is protected and stabilized by both ligaments and muscles. It serves two crucial but contradictory functions: mobility and stability. To give the arm a large range of motion, the shoulder must be extremely flexible—as seen, for example, in a baseball pitcher's windup. At the same time, to help us move heavy objects (furniture, for example), the shoulder must provide a strong and stable fixed point that allows us to push and pull. To enable this variety of movements, the shoulder contains multiple bursae (sacs) that secrete synovial fluid to reduce friction in the joint and around the soft tissues.

All movements of the shoulder involve the scapula, which is commonly referred to as the shoulder blade. Several muscles attach to the scapula, but few of them are considered major. One of the major muscles is the trapezius, whose main function can be seen when you shrug your shoulders. The muscle's functions also include elevating and depressing the shoulder blades away from the trunk. We elevate and depress the shoulder blades every time we lift something over our head and every time we safely lower something to the floor.

The deltoid muscle also connects to the scapula and is responsible for many movements, including changing the angle of the shoulder joint. The deltoid is a bulky muscle and is the most commonly recognized shoulder muscle. Because of its rounded shape, it acts as a shock absorber for the shoulder joint, and it also aids in many arm movements. These movements are also enabled by the fact that the shoulder is a ball-and-socket joint that can rotate in many directions.

Despite being the most widely known shoulder muscle, the deltoid is not the most commonly injured one. That distinction goes to the rotator cuff, which is a group of four short muscles with about the width of a shoelace. These four muscles pull the upper arm bone—the humerus—into the socket and attach to and strengthen the joint as a whole. The rotator cuff muscles surround the head of the humerus and stabilize it in the glenoid fossa, which serves as the joint's socket. If the humerus were not anchored by the rotator cuff, it would be much more prone to dislocation.

We can think of this joint in terms of a seal holding a ball on his or her nose. The head of the humerus acts as a ball that fits into the glenoid fossa in much the same manner as the ball sits on the seal's nose. Without the rotator cuff muscles, the ball would slip off of the seal's nose much more often. As a result, injury to the rotator cuff is debilitating because it completely disables the movement patterns of the upper arm. To make matters worse, the other muscles of the shoulder and arm also lose their ability to move the upper arm correctly, which means that a rotator cuff injury is often accompanied by a shoulder dislocation.

Other muscles that act on the shoulder joint but do not attach to the scapula are the latissimus dorsi and the pectoralis major. You may be familiar with these two as the large muscle running down your back (latissimus dorsi) and the large triangular chest muscle (pectoralis major). They do not originate on the shoulder blade but connect instead to the axial skeleton or trunk. They work together during various movements, such as push-ups and pull-ups.

The muscles acting on the shoulder joint and shoulder girdle work in combination, which makes it difficult to locate a single muscle responsible for a given activity or exercise. On the other hand, these muscles are easy to stretch and strengthen because of the joint's mobility. However, this mobility also means that the joint is stable in some positions but vulnerable in others.

The shoulder is in its most vulnerable position when it is in flexion—that is, when the angle of the joint is shortened. The shoulder is in flexion, for example, when you push a sofa across the floor with your arms straight out in front of you. Another example can be seen when a swimmer does the backstroke, during which the arm comes out of the water, passes over the head, and then cuts back into the water.

Generally, then, shoulder injuries are common in throwing sports and activities that involve pushing. Shoulder dislocations often occur when the shoulder is in a flexed position and a sudden force is applied to the upper arm bone (the humerus). For example, traumatic injury can occur when a person reaches out to catch something that is falling or thrusts an arm out to break a fall.

COMMON INJURIES OF THE SHOULDER JOINT

Common shoulder injuries include shoulder instability, shoulder strains and sprains, and rotator cuff strains and impingement. Shoulder instability is usually caused by a blow to the shoulder, a throwing injury, or a fall on an outstretched arm. If surgery is not needed, the problem can be addressed by strengthening and stretching through a gradually increasing range of motion. Chronic or long-lasting instability causes a gradual onset of muscle weakness and progressively damages the shoulder structures on the front of the deltoid muscle.

Shoulder instability can occur in either the front (anterior) or the back (posterior) portion of the shoulder joint. The location affects the recommended rehabilitation exercises. Therefore, the two locations are treated separately in the exercise listings provided at the end of this chapter.

Shoulder strains and sprains occur in the soft-tissue structures of the deltoid, such as the bursae and the rotator cuff. Strains usually affect the ligaments that attach bone to bone, whereas sprains affect the muscles and connecting tendons. These injuries may cause localized pain in the shoulder joint and may radiate down the arm. The pain increases during movements involving the specific tissues—for example, reaching over the head, lifting an object, or stretching through a full range of motion.

Rotator cuff strains and impingement are common in athletes who use an overhead or overarm rotating motion; examples include baseball pitchers and swimmers. These problems are also seen in professions such as construction workers, factory workers, or heavy machine operators, that involve repetitive overhead movement. These injuries are often serious and may require surgery.

During rehabilitation, rotator cuff movements should be smooth and free of sharp pain. Even when exercising for overall health benefits, it is best to err on the conservative side and keep your resistance light so that your musculature is not overloaded. In an aquatic environment, it may be beneficial to begin rehabilitation by simply moving the joint through the water without using any additional surface-area or drag equipment (such as webbed gloves, buoys, or a pool noodle).

EXERCISES FOR SHOULDER REHABILITATION

Each of the injuries described in this chapter requires a unique rehabilitation sequence. As a result, the following charts are individualized according to condition. Because the muscles that move the shoulder joint are all intricately connected, you should start with a small range of motion to see how the joint operates as a whole. If you feel any sharp pain in the joint or bony structures during an exercise, omit that particular activity. On the other hand, discomfort in a muscle or soft tissue simply means that you are getting stronger, and in this case it is okay to progress slowly.

The exercises in this chapter are designed to be completed in the order listed in the chart. The initial exercises of each section will activate the muscles surrounding the shoulder joint. The beginning exercises begin with a rotation so that the shoulder is prepared for any rotational movement that may occur in the back stretch. In the intermediate and advanced sections, the rotations will activate the muscles so they are prepared for exercises that require the circular motion of the muscles surrounding the shoulder.

Table 12.1   Exercises for Anterior Shoulder Instability

Shoulder exercises		Sets and reps or duration
Beginning exercises		
4.17 Internal shoulder rotation (p. 59)		2 or 3 sets of 8–10 reps without equipment
Warm-up: back stretch (chapter 3) (p. 30)		2 or 3 sets of 30 seconds
Intermediate exercises		
4.17 Internal shoulder rotation (p. 59)		2 or 3 sets of 8–10 reps with webbed glove
5.18 Anchored jab punch (p. 83)		2 or 3 sets of 30 seconds
5.19 Anchored arm chaos (p. 84)		2 or 3 sets of 30 seconds

Shoulder exercises		Sets and reps or duration
Intermediate exercises *(continued)*		
Warm-up: back stretch (chapter 3) (p. 30)		2 or 3 sets of 45 seconds
Advanced exercises		
4.17 Internal shoulder rotation (p. 59)		2 or 3 sets of 8–10 reps with buoy
5.18 Anchored jab punch (p. 83)		2 or 3 sets of 1 minute
5.19 Anchored arm chaos (p. 84)		2 or 3 sets of 1 minute
6.18 Triceps push-up (p. 117)		2 or 3 sets of 8–10 reps

(continued)

Table 12.1 Exercises for Anterior Shoulder Instability *(continued)*

Shoulder exercises		Sets and reps or duration
Advanced exercises *(continued)*		
6.19 Spiderman crawl (p. 118)		2 or 3 sets of 8–10 reps
Warm-up: back stretch (chapter 3) (p. 30)		2 or 3 sets of 1 minute

Table 12.2 Exercises for Posterior Shoulder Instability

Shoulder stability exercises		Sets and reps or duration
Beginning exercises		
4.18 External shoulder rotation (p. 60)		2 or 3 sets of 8–10 reps with no equipment
Warm-up: standing chest opener (chapter 3) (p. 30)		2 or 3 sets of 30 seconds
Intermediate exercises		
4.18 External shoulder rotation (p. 60)		2 or 3 sets of 8–10 reps with webbed gloves
Warm-up: standing chest opener (chapter 3) (p. 30)		2 or 3 sets of 45 seconds

(continued)

Table 12.2 Exercises for Posterior Shoulder Instability *(continued)*

Shoulder stability exercises	Sets and reps or duration
Advanced exercises	
4.18 External shoulder rotation (p. 60)	2 or 3 sets of 8–10 reps with buoy
Warm-up: standing chest opener (chapter 3) (p. 30)	2 or 3 sets of 1 minute

Table 12.3 Exercises for Rotator Cuff Strain

Rotator cuff exercises		Sets and reps or duration
Beginning exercises		
4.17 Internal shoulder rotation (p. 59)		2 or 3 sets of 8–10 reps without equipment
4.18 External shoulder rotation (p. 60)		2 or 3 sets of 8–10 reps without equipment
5.18 Anchored jab punch (p. 83)		2 or 3 sets of 30 seconds
5.19 Anchored arm chaos (p. 84)		2 or 3 sets of 30 seconds
Warm-up: back stretch (chapter 3) (p. 30)		2 or 3 sets of 30 seconds

(continued)

Table 12.3 Exercises for Rotator Cuff Strain *(continued)*

Rotator cuff exercises	Sets and reps or duration
Intermediate exercises	
4.17 Internal shoulder rotation (p. 59)	2 or 3 sets of 8–10 reps with webbed glove
4.18 External shoulder rotation (p. 60)	2 or 3 sets of 8–10 reps with webbed glove
5.18 Anchored jab punch (p. 83)	2 or 3 sets of 1 minute
5.19 Anchored arm chaos (p. 84)	2 or 3 sets of 1 minute
5.26 Chest press (p. 91)	2 or 3 sets of 8–10 reps

Rotator cuff exercises		Sets and reps or duration
Intermediate exercises *(continued)*		
5.27 Straight-arm push-down (p. 92)		2 or 3 sets of 8–10 reps
Warm-up: back stretch (chapter 3) (p. 30)		2 or 3 sets of 1 minute
Advanced exercises		
4.17 Internal shoulder rotation (p. 59)		2 or 3 sets of 8–10 reps with buoy
4.18 External shoulder rotation (p. 60)		2 or 3 sets of 8–10 reps with buoy
5.26 Chest press (p. 91)		2 or 3 sets of 12–15 reps

(continued)

Table 12.3 Exercises for Rotator Cuff Strain *(continued)*

Rotator cuff exercises		Sets and reps or duration
Advanced exercises *(continued)*		
5.27 Straight-arm push-down (p. 92)		2 or 3 sets of 12–15 reps
5.29 Wall push-up (p. 94)		2 or 3 sets of 8–10 reps
6.18 Triceps push-up (p. 117)		2 or 3 sets of 8–10 reps
6.19 Spiderman crawl (p. 118)		2 or 3 sets of 8–10 reps
Warm-up: back stretch (chapter 3) (p. 30)		2 or 3 sets of 1 minute

CHAPTER 13

ELBOW AND WRIST JOINTS

The elbow is a fairly stable hinge joint where the humerus of the upper arm joins with the two bones of the lower arm, which are the ulna and the radius. The elbow joint is limited to two movements—bending and straightening. Thus it is a rather simple joint that decreases or increases the surface areas of the arm and forearm as it bends, an action that involves both the ulna and the humerus. The radius is involved in turning over the palm (through supination and pronation) and therefore is more closely associated with the wrist joint.

The rotation of the wrist joint (through supination and pronation) involves the relationship of the bones in the forearm—the ulna and radius. Depending on which way your palm is facing, one of these bones crosses over the other. Overuse of the wrist joint often occurs in work-related tasks and may result in tendon or ligament injuries. If your career requires a repetitive wrist movement, you are more likely to experience an overuse injury due to repeated stress on the joint. There are steps you can take to minimize stress to the wrist joint. If at all possible, reduce the speed and force of repetitive movements, take frequent breaks, and try to change the position of the wrist during the work day.

Elbow and wrist problems often involve overuse, fall-related fractures, or arthritis. They can be minor or serious, and they often involve pain, swelling, numbness, tingling, weakness, and a decrease in the range of motion. Many of these injuries occur during contact activities, such as wrestling, football, and lacrosse. A number of elbow injuries are also caused by high-speed activities, such as biking, skateboarding, and field hockey.

As we get older, it is more likely for these injuries to involve a fracture because our bones are becoming fragile. We are also more likely to fall and make contact with a hard surface because our vision and balance decline with age. Treatments for such injuries may include first aid, application of a brace or cast, physical therapy, and, in extreme cases, surgery.

COMMON ELBOW AND WRIST INJURIES

Common elbow injuries include epicondylitis, carpal tunnel syndrome, fracture of the elbow or wrist (or even of the ulna, radius, or humerus), injury of the ulnar collateral ligament, elbow bursitis ("Popeye elbow"), and muscle tears or ruptures. Epicondylitis, or "golfer's elbow," involves microdamage to tissue due to overuse in activities such as gardening, carpentry, and swinging sports. It appears in two forms, both of which involve overuse injuries of the muscles in the wrist and lower arm. Lateral epicondylitis, often referred to as "tennis elbow," is associated with activities in which the wrist is repetitively extended. The sufferer feels soreness or pain on the outside of the elbow due to overuse of the forearm muscles. Medial epicondylitis occurs when the wrist is repetitively flexed—for example, by carrying a heavy suitcase. This form, which is less common than tennis elbow, causes soreness or pain in the inner part of the elbow.

Both kinds of epicondylitis are characterized by gradual onset due to a lack of strength, power, endurance, or flexibility in the wrist muscles. Therefore, any exercise that gradually increases the endurance of the involved muscles can help prevent these problems. Once an overuse injury has occurred, most health care professionals recommend following the PRICE acronym—protect during activity, rest when possible, ice, compress, and elevate when needed—and then gradually returning to activity.

Carpal tunnel syndrome is a common compression syndrome of the wrist. It involves inflammation, usually due to repetitive motion, that compresses the nerve canal and thus exerts pressure on the median nerve. This pressure results in pain, weakness, and numbness in the hand. It may be released through immobilization, physical therapy, surgery, or a combination approach.

Elbow and wrist fractures—as well as fractures of the ulna, radius, and humerus—cause sharp pain in the affected joint or bone. After taking X-rays, the physician typically immobilizes the area with a cast. Many fractures require surgery and physical therapy, after which you can begin a rehabilitation program in the pool to strengthen the muscles attached to the affected bone or joint.

Injuries of the ulnar collateral ligament can be a setback for anyone. These injuries can range from a mild sprain to a complete tear. A completely torn ligament requires surgery and physical therapy before you can begin rehabilitation in the pool.

Bursitis on the elbow is often referred to as "Popeye elbow" due to the swelling behind the elbow joint. It can be caused by gout, rheumatoid arthritis, or a localized infection. Bursitis can be painful, but you can usually take care of it by using the PRICE acronym: protect, rest, ice, compress, and elevate.

Muscle tears or ruptures in the upper arm can involve either the biceps or the triceps. When this type of injury happens, the muscle rolls up into a ball. In some cases, it reattaches on its own with rest. In other cases, it must be reattached surgically. The recommended course of treatment depends on age, activity level, and physician's advice.

EXERCISES FOR ELBOW AND WRIST REHABILITATION

Rehabilitation of the elbow or wrist can be a difficult process because symptoms can reappear when the injured area is used. After a period of rest, it may be time to simply strengthen the muscles, tendons, and ligaments surrounding the affected joint. Once the swelling goes down, begin by increasing your range of motion, which can be aided by any movement in the pool that uses the joints in your arm. You can then add exercises that put weight on the joint or increase the gripping motion performed with your hands, fingers, and wrists. Remember the basic rule: pain in a joint may mean that you need to consult with a physician, whereas pain in a muscle simply means that you are activating the fibers of that muscle.

Table 13.1 Exercises for Elbow and Wrist Rehabilitation

Elbow and wrist exercises		Sets and reps or duration
Beginning exercises		
Warm-up: standing chest opener (chapter 3) (p. 30)		2 or 3 sets of 30 seconds
5.18 Anchored jab punch (p. 83)		2 or 3 sets of 30 seconds
5.19 Anchored arm chaos (p. 84)		2 or 3 sets of 30 seconds
Warm-up: back stretch (chapter 3) (p. 30)		2 or 3 sets of 30 seconds
Intermediate exercises		
Warm-up: standing chest opener (chapter 3) (p. 30)		2 or 3 sets of 45 seconds

Elbow and wrist exercises	Sets and reps or duration
Intermediate exercises *(continued)*	
5.18 Anchored jab punch (p. 83) 	2 or 3 sets of 45 seconds
5.19 Anchored arm chaos (p. 84) 	2 or 3 sets of 45 seconds
Warm-up: back stretch (chapter 3) (p. 30) 	2 or 3 sets of 45 seconds
5.26 Chest press (p. 91) 	2 or 3 sets of 8–10 reps
5.27 Straight-arm push-down (p. 92) 	2 or 3 sets of 8–10 reps

(continued)

Table 13.1 Exercises for Elbow and Wrist Rehabilitation *(continued)*.

Elbow and wrist exercises		Sets and reps or duration
Advanced exercises		
Warm-up: standing chest opener (chapter 3) (p. 30)		2 or 3 sets of 1 minute
5.18 Anchored jab punch (p. 83)		2 or 3 sets of 1 minute
5.19 Anchored arm chaos (p. 84)		2 or 3 sets of 1 minute
Warm-up: back stretch (chapter 3) (p. 30)		2 or 3 sets of 1 minute
5.26 Chest press (p. 91)		2 or 3 sets of 12–15 reps

Elbow and wrist exercises	Sets and reps or duration
Advanced exercises *(continued)*	
5.27 Straight-arm push-down (p. 92) 	2 or 3 sets of 12–15 reps
5.29 Wall push-up (p. 94) 	2 or 3 sets of 8–10 reps
6.18 Triceps push-up (p. 117) 	2 or 3 sets of 8–10 reps
6.19 Spiderman crawl (p. 118) 	2 or 3 sets of 8–10 reps

PART IV

WATER EXERCISE PROGRAMS

This final section of *Water Exercise* addresses three main topics: general workouts for healthy populations, cross-training programs for advanced participants, and workouts for special populations. Chapter 14 presents water workouts for individuals who prefer simple, efficient programs that can be completed in 30 to 45 minutes. The workouts are effective and target muscles throughout the body, including the heart. Over time, you should see a decrease in your resting heart rate, an increase in your muscle tone, an increase in your cardiovascular endurance, and a decrease in many of your blood counts (for example, total cholesterol, LDL cholesterol, and triglycerides). As your fitness level improves, the length of your workout should gradually increase.

Chapter 15 is designed for healthy adults who already participate in an exercise program. Integrating water exercises into your program decreases your chance of overtraining in activities that involve a great amount of impact, decreases your risk of getting bored with exercise, and helps prevent your body from hitting a plateau. The programs presented in chapter 15 can all be completed in an hour or less, and they may include movements in both the shallow and the deep end of the pool.

Chapter 16 is designed for individuals with considerations that are not necessarily injuries but that still affect the choice of which water exercises are appropriate. The goals for these exercises differ from the goals for exercises described in the rehabilitation chapters. The main goal here is to increase your fitness level while maintaining safety within the parameters of your specific condition. The sample programs presented here can accommodate needs that are specific to pregnancy, neuromuscular disease, and autoimmune disease.

Whether you are looking to maintain a level of fitness, increase your fitness level, or find specific modifications for one of these particular conditions, you will find what you are looking for in this final section—complete with charts and directives. Whichever program you undertake, warm up before you begin. The most effective warm-up always involves doing the same things you will do in the workout but at a lower intensity. In addition, water walking, water jogging, and deep-water running are always great activities for increasing heart rate, blood pressure, rate of breathing, and blood flow to working muscles.

When you complete your workout, perform static stretching. These stretches, which you hold for a short period of time, are explained with photographs in chapter 3. If you feel your body getting cold while you hold a static stretch, move other parts of your body. For example, if you are stretching your upper back with your hands clasped in front of your body, walk through the water. This kind of movement helps keep your blood flowing and your body warm.

CHAPTER 14

BASIC WATER FITNESS

Any fitness program, whether performed on land or in water, should address all of the components of health-related fitness: cardiovascular endurance, muscular endurance, muscular strength, and flexibility. To meet these goals, this chapter presents a basic water exercise routine that incorporates movements for all of the major muscles at an intensity that challenges your heart. As mentioned in chapter 3, flexibility naturally comes into play as you contract opposing muscles. For example, if you perform rebounding knee lifts, the muscles in the front of your legs contract while the muscles in the back of your legs stretch. In addition, the buoyancy and resistance provided by water make our muscles contract regardless of whether the leg is being raised or lowered (gravity is not such a factor in the water).

For any workout you choose from this chapter, your warm-up can consist either of exercises presented in chapter 3 or of shallow-water walking or jogging. In addition, remember to use your upper body by moving your arms just as you would if walking or jogging down the street. Three to five minutes of water walking or jogging generally suffices for a warm-up unless the water is unusually cold. You will know that it is time to move on to the main workout when the initial chill of the water disappears and your joints feel free to move through larger ranges of motion. Your breathing may also speed up a bit as you intensify your movements.

Equipment should be avoided during the warm-up segment because it could increase the surface area of a moving limb before your muscles are prepared to work that hard. If you prefer to put your webbed gloves on while your hands are still dry, just remember to move your hands through the water as if they were slicing—not pushing—during your warm-up movements. In other words, move your hands as if they were the nose of a speedboat rather than the square front of a pontoon boat. As you get warm, you can gradually change some moves to a push.

Your workout will be more effective if you keep moving from one exercise to the other. For this reason, we have sequenced the basic exercises presented here in a way that allows one move to flow into the next without having to stop your feet and readjust your body. You can choose to do as many repetitions as you would like before you move on to the next move, and you can do sets of multiple reps of two sequenced moves. For instance, you might do eight jumping jacks followed by eight cross-countries and then eight tuck jumps, and you could perform the sequence three or four times.

The table of exercises presented in this chapter gives you some options for increasing your intensity. For example, you might choose to move the tuck jumps forward for eight counts in one iteration and backward for eight counts in the next. The basic rule to follow is this: The more you move your body through the water in different directions, the harder your heart and muscles work, which means that you burn more calories for energy.

The following programs are arranged in a way that allows room for individual preferences. For example, if you would like to repeat one program multiple times after your warm-up exercises, that is fine. Similarly, if you would like to link two beginning routines together, that is also fine.

Each beginning routine lasts about 10 minutes, including the warm-up and the final flexibility stretches. As your fitness level improves, you might choose to link a beginning program to the intermediate program, which lasts about 12 minutes. You might then progress to linking two intermediate routines for a total of 24 minutes. The advanced routines are designed to last about 15 minutes each.

Every person has his or her own fitness level; in addition, personal preferences range from favoring a limited set of choices to favoring more variation. Regardless of such choices, you should aim to exercise in the water every other day, or three or four times per week. For example, you could do one routine on Monday and another on Wednesday and the one you did on Monday could be done again on Friday, for a total of three. Consistency in your frequency is more important than the frequency with which you perform a particular routine, so just have fun while using the tables as a guide.

Table 14.1   Beginning Routine 1

Exercise	Intermediate options	Advanced options
4.5 Calf raise (p. 43)	—	—
4.9 Pop jump (p. 48)	Change to 5.11 tuck jump. (p. 75)	Move forward and backward.
4.6 Squat (p. 44)	Change to 5.20 side squat. (p. 85)	—
4.8 Jumping jack (p. 46)	Move right and left.	Move forward and backward.
4.13 Biceps curl (p. 55)	—	—

(continued)

Table 14.1 Beginning Routine 1 *(continued)*

Exercise	Intermediate options	Advanced options
4.16 Rebounding knee lift (p. 58)	Move forward.	Move forward and backward.
4.3 Hip extension (p. 41)	—	—
4.10 Cross-country ski (p. 50)	Move forward.	Move right and left.
5.18 Anchored jab punch (p. 83)	—	—
4.4 Leg swing (p. 42)	Change to 6.6 rebounding leg swing. (p. 103)	Move either forward and back or right and left.

Exercise	Intermediate options	Advanced options
5.21 Walking lunge (p. 86)	—	Add a rebound, make jumping lunges, and change the front foot while your feet are suspended in the water.

Table 14.2 Beginning Routine 2

Exercise	Intermediate options	Advanced options
4.1 Knee flexion and extension (p. 39)	Change to 5.25 single-leg press. (p. 90)	Change to 6.9 double-leg push-down. (p. 106)
5.13 Neutral jack (p. 77)	—	Change to 6.7 suspended jack. (p. 104)
5.16 Carioca (p. 80)	Change to 5.17 serpentine running. (p. 82)	—
4.2 Hip flexion (p. 40)	Change to 5.1 straight-leg kick to the front. (p. 63)	Change to 6.6 rebounding leg swing. (p. 103)
5.19 Anchored arm chaos (p. 84)	—	—

Exercise	Intermediate options	Advanced options
4.14 Noodle bicycle riding (p. 56) 	Ride the noodle in shapes to challenge balance (e.g., circle, figure 8).	—
4.11 Trunk rotation (p. 52) 	—	—
4.12 Triceps push-down (p. 54) 	—	—
4.2 Hip flexion (p. 40) 	Change to 5.1 straight-leg kick to the front. (p. 63) 	Change to 5.15 hurdle leap moving forward. (p. 79) 
4.3 Hip extension (p. 41) 	Change to 5.8 rear kick. (p. 70) 	—

(continued)

Table 14.2 Beginning Routine 2 *(continued)*

Exercise	Intermediate options	Advanced options
5.9 Criss-cross jumping jack (p. 72)	Change to 5.10 star jack. (p. 74)	Change to 6.4 power jack. (p. 101)

Table 14.3 Intermediate Routine

Exercise		Advanced options
5.2 Rocking horse (p. 64)		Move right and left as you rock forward and backward.
5.5 Pendulum (p. 67)		Move forward and backward as you move like a pendulum from side to side.
5.3 Side mogul (p. 65)		Add a leg tuck to the chest as you change sides.
5.4 Twisting mogul (p. 66)		Add a leg tuck as you twist from side to side.
5.6 Soccer kick (p. 68)		Move from right to left as you kick.

(continued)

Table 14.3 Intermediate Routine *(continued)*

Exercise	Advanced options
5.7 Hoedown kick (p. 69)	Change to 6.3 side leap. (p. 100)
5.13 Neutral jack (p. 77)	Alternate with 8 counts of 6.2 crooked jack. (p. 99)
5.11 Tuck jump (p. 75)	Alternate with 8 counts of 6.1 frog jump. (p. 98)
5.12 Front-to-back mogul (p. 76)	Add a leg tuck as you jump from front to back.
5.14 Neutral cross-country (p. 78)	Alternate with 8 counts of 5.15 hurdle leap. (p. 79)

Exercise	Advanced options
5.26 Chest press (p. 91)	Change to 6.14 stationary plank. (p. 113)
5.29 Wall push-up (p. 94)	Change to 6.18 triceps push-up. (p. 117)
5.18 Anchored jab punch (p. 83)	Alternate with 1 minute of 5.19 anchored arm chaos. (p. 84)
5.22 Straight-leg zombie walk (p. 87)	Alternate with 8 counts of 5.23 tightrope traveling. (p. 88)
5.27 Straight-arm push-down (p. 92)	Alternate with 8 counts of 5.30 prone hip abduction and adduction. (p. 95)

CHAPTER 15

ADVANCED CROSS-TRAINING

This chapter presents advanced training options for individuals who have been training consistently and now seek to increase their fitness level or add cross-training options. For people who usually train on land, cross-training in the pool offers several benefits. First, it subjects your joints to less stress, thus decreasing your risk of injury. It also adds variation to your workout, which helps you stay mentally engaged in your program; boredom is frequently cited as a reason by people who drop out of an exercise program. Cross-training also subjects your body to different stimuli, which makes you less likely to hit a plateau in your fitness progression.

Because this chapter addresses advanced training, it presents exercises that differ in type from those presented in chapter 14. Specifically, the exercises described in chapter 14 focus on aerobic training, during which your body constantly uses oxygen to help turn the food you have eaten into available energy in the form of adenosine triphosphate (ATP). In contrast, this chapter presents some progressions that take you into the anaerobic training zone. You can tell when you are working at the top of your aerobic zone and moving into the anaerobic zone because your breathing becomes labored and your mouth falls open in an attempt to increase your rate of respiration.

Anaerobic training is more intense, but the length of time for which you stay breathless is short—usually 30 to 90 seconds. You can use a stopwatch or lap clock to determine how long you can work anaerobically, or without oxygen. Then engage in a recovery period in which you slow down your activity, which will slow your breathing and focus on inhaling as opposed to exhaling. This type of exercise is called interval training because it intersperses short bursts of high-intensity activity with periods of low-intensity activity during which you recover actively while you continue to move. As a result, your heart rate and respirations will change in intensity several times when you use the programs presented in this chapter.

Interval training provides several benefits. The most obvious and easily understood benefit is that you burn more calories during interval training than during steady-state aerobic training. Because your work intensity is higher at certain times during interval training, your body must break down more molecules of ATP to enable your muscle fibers to contract more rapidly. This process requires the breakdown of food substances, which requires energy in the form of heat, otherwise known as a calorie.

Because your work intensity increases, your muscle fibers must contract more rapidly and with more power. This is the function of a kind of muscle fiber referred to as a fast-twitch fiber, which is one of three basic types of fibers found in our muscles. Fast-twitch muscle fibers contract rapidly with a great deal of force, but they fatigue rapidly. In contrast, slow-twitch fibers are also slow to fatigue but do not produce as much power. Intermediate fibers possess characteristics of both fast-twitch and slow-twitch fibers. When you work anaerobically, you recruit a large number of fast-twitch fibers that are anaerobic, which means that they do not require oxygen. Slow-twitch muscle fibers do require oxygen, so you use them when your work intensity drops while you perform active aerobic recovery.

As we age, we lose fast-twitch muscle fibers if we do not use them; therefore, another benefit of interval training is that it helps preserve these fibers. In addition, when you use the powerful fast-twitch fibers, they pull on your tendons with a great deal of force, which helps strengthen your bones. This strengthening helps prevent brittle bones as you age.

Yet another benefit of anaerobic training involves a process called excess postexercise oxygen consumption (EPOC), which, simply put, is the restoration of the body to homeostasis or equilibrium after an intense workout. Because the body is using energy, or calories, in this restoration process, EPOC plays a role in weight management. In short, it's an extra burst of calorie burning after your workout.

This phenomenon happens only after an intense workout during which you cross your anaerobic threshold, use your fast-twitch muscle fibers, and become breathless. Therefore, it is not something that beginners or individuals with an injury or special condition should practice without clearance from a health care provider. In addition, always remember to begin with three to five minutes of gentle water walking as a warm-up and to conclude with basic stretches from chapter 3 for your flexibility segment.

Now that you know the benefits of cross-training and of crossing the anaerobic threshold, you can use the workouts presented in the following tables to take your fitness to the next level. Each workout lasts less than 30 minutes due to the intensity of the work. Think of your body as a race car: the faster and more powerful the engine, the shorter the race. In addition, your gas tank may empty faster than that of a slower car!

You are not limited to the workouts presented in the tables. You can also create your own workout using any of the exercises presented in chapters 4 through 7. To go breathless, perform the exercises powerfully with large movements and a slight increase in speed. You should aim to stay breathless in one particular exercise for anywhere from 30 to 90 seconds. Then you should do an active recovery by performing a beginning exercise for double the amount of time that you were breathless. For example, if you do power jacks for 30 seconds, follow them with 60 seconds of regular jumping jacks for active recovery.

As your heart becomes fitter and fitter, you will be able to remain breathless for longer and recover more quickly. At that point, try to use a one-to-one ratio of breathlessness to recovery. For instance, you might do intense deep-water running for one minute, then recover for one minute by doing deep-water leg circles. The options are endless, as long as you remember to stage the workout in intervals of intense work mixed with less intense periods of recovery.

Table 15.1 Shallow-Water Workout

Aerobic recovery exercises for 30–90 seconds	Intense anaerobic exercises for 30–90 seconds (with an increase in power)
4.8 Jumping jack (p.46)	5.1 Straight-leg kick to the front (p. 63)
4.10 Cross-country ski (p. 50)	5.3 Side mogul (p. 65)
4.16 Rebounding knee lift (p. 58)	5.7 Hoedown kick (p. 69)
5.4 Twisting mogul (p. 66)	5.11 Tuck jump (p. 75)
5.2 Rocking horse (p. 64)	5.12 Front-to-back mogul (p. 76)

Aerobic recovery exercises for 30–90 seconds	Intense anaerobic exercises for 30–90 seconds (with an increase in power)
5.5 Pendulum (p. 67) 	6.1 Frog jump (p. 98) 
5.6 Soccer kick (p. 68) 	6.5 Rocket (p. 102) 
5.15 Hurdle leap (p. 79) 	6.4 Power jack (p. 101) 
5.14 Neutral cross-country (p. 78) 	6.8 Suspended eggbeater (p. 105) 

Table 15.2   Deep-Water Workout

Aerobic recovery exercises for 30–90 seconds		Intense anaerobic exercises for 30–90 seconds (with an increase in power)	
6.10 Side shoot-through (p. 107)		7.1 Deep-water flotation jack (p. 123)	
6.11 Front and back shoot-through (p. 108)		7.2 Deep-water flotation cross-country (p. 124)	
6.12 Flotation extension and abduction-adduction (p. 110)		7.3 Deep-water running (p. 125)	
7.5 Deep-water walking stick (p. 127)		7.4 Deep-water rope jump (p. 126)	
7.6 Free-hanging leg circle (p. 128)		5.4 Twisting mogul (with noodle around waist) (p. 66)	

Aerobic recovery exercises for 30–90 seconds		Intense anaerobic exercises for 30–90 seconds (with an increase in power)	
7.7 Deep-water seated core (p. 129)		6.9 Double-leg push-down (in deep water) (p. 106)	
6.13 Noodle balance (in deep water)* (p. 112)		7.3 Deep-water running (p. 125)	
6.14 Stationary plank (in deep water)* (p. 113)		7.2 Deep-water flotation cross-country (p. 124)	

*For the aerobic recovery with 6.13, the noodle balance, and 6.14, the stationary plank, the exercises will be done in deep water with the head remaining above the water so the noodle will be suspended in the deep water. The stationary plank will be done with the body at the same angle, but the toes are pointed down to the bottom of the pool. Remember, this is an advanced workout and these exercises are challenging.

CHAPTER 16

SPECIAL POPULATIONS

This chapter helps you identify appropriate water exercises if you have a condition affecting not just one area but the body as a whole. Therefore, the workout options presented here differ from the injury-specific workouts discussed in other chapters. Specific conditions addressed in this chapter include pregnancy, multiple sclerosis, Parkinson's disease, muscular dystrophy, fibromyalgia, and rheumatoid arthritis. Exercise goals also differ for each individual within a particular population. In all cases, however, it is important for you to review any program with your health care provider and obtain clearance before you begin to exercise.

PREGNANCY

Pregnancy is a natural and beautiful part of a woman's life, yet exercising while pregnant often challenges our comfort level. As pregnancy progresses, physiological changes affect our heart rate, posture, and movement patterns. Indeed, carrying and feeding another human being in one's body stresses all of the regulatory systems even while the body is at rest.

One of the first physiological changes produced by pregnancy is an increase in the resting heart rate. The heart must work harder to provide oxygen and nutrients through the bloodstream for both the woman's and the baby's body. Because the heart rate increases naturally during pregnancy, you will not be able to rely on that number to calculate the intensity of your workout. As a result, the best way to measure intensity is through what is called the rate of perceived exertion. This approach uses a scale of 1 to 10, in which 1 equates to relaxing on the sofa and 10 means you cannot push any harder.

On this scale, a workout should rate between a 6 and an 8, depending on how far along you are in your pregnancy. If you were already exercising in the water before conception, your first-trimester workouts can push toward an exertion rating of 8 because your body is used to exercise stressors. If you were not exercising before conception, start at a lower intensity, closer to an exertion rating of 6. As the baby grows and the weight of the woman's body increases, it will take less work for you to reach the same numbers. As a result, you will need to stay near the lower end of the exertion range (that is, near an exertion rating of 6) as the pregnancy progresses into the third trimester.

Another change that affects aquatic activity is the redistribution of adipose or fat tissue around the torso or belly area. This increase in fat makes your body more buoyant. As a result, you float more easily, and your belly rises at a slightly different tempo than the rest of your body, which makes jumping uncomfortable. For this reason, many of the jumping or rebounding exercises presented in the earlier chapters are omitted from this workout program. Instead, the majority of exercises are neutral, anchored, or suspended.

If you find that a move is impeded by the size of your growing belly, simply reposition your leg so that the hip joint has a greater range of motion. For example, instead of kicking directly to the front, open the kick slightly to the side. You will still strengthen the muscles of the hip but at a different angle.

Of course, your weight will increase during pregnancy as well, but buoyancy allows you to work out with only about one-tenth of your actual weight—a true bonus as your abdomen grows! This benefit reduces stress on your bones (which are already carrying more weight due to the baby) and therefore reduces your risk of injury. Just remember to enter and exit the pool carefully, using the handrails, because your growing abdomen makes you more likely to lose your balance.

The most dangerous change during pregnancy is the increase in heat generated by the body. Your body is now doing for two people everything that it used to do for one, and this double duty includes oxidizing food for energy. You are also pumping blood for two people and cooling down two bodies, which makes overheating a great concern during physical activity of any sort. In this regard, the pool is a great environment because the body dissipates heat into the cooler water. Remember, however, that if you exercise in a therapeutic pool with a temperature higher than the mid-80s Fahrenheit (roughly 30 degrees Celsius), it will be more difficult for your body to cool the body of the baby.

Pregnancy also causes an increase in a hormone called relaxin. This hormone is always present in a female's body in small amounts, but it increases as the body readies itself to open the hip region and give birth. This increase affects the flexibility of the connective tissues, such as tendons and ligaments. For this reason, pregnant women need to stretch only gently, without applying too much pressure on a joint to increase its range of motion. The pool is a safe environment for stretching if you just let the buoyancy of the water lift your limbs without applying extra force with your hands.

Another common physiological change brought on by pregnancy is bloating or edema. Fortunately, the hydrostatic pressure of water, especially deep water, causes water in the body to exit the spaces between the cells and enter the bloodstream. From there, it passes through the kidneys and is excreted in urine if the body is well hydrated.

MULTIPLE SCLEROSIS

Multiple sclerosis (MS) is a degenerative disease that generally affects people in young adulthood and is more common among women. It progresses at varying rates and involves a loss of myelin or tissue in the central nervous system, particularly the brain and spinal cord. The exact cause is not known, but MS is thought to be an autoimmune disease in which the body periodically turns upon itself, thus causing damage to the myelin sheath and scar tissue or sclerosis.

Many people with MS benefit from a regular exercise program. Aquatic exercises should be done in a cooler pool—specifically, in the upper 70s to low 80s Fahrenheit (about 25 to 28 degrees Celsius). Care should be taken when exiting or entering the pool due to possible double vision or an atypical walking pattern. Aquatic exercises should be done in the shallow end for added stability and to increase weight-bearing activity. Feeling the bottom of the pool also helps improve sensory input. Exercises that improve walking patterns such as walking lunges (5.21), the straight-leg zombie walk (5.22), and tightrope traveling (5.23) will be beneficial for patients with MS. These exercises strengthen the muscles that help provide a proper gait pattern.

PARKINSON'S DISEASE

In Parkinson's disease, certain neurons in the brain fail to secrete dopamine, a neurotransmitter. Symptoms include muscle tremors and rigidity, as well as emotional issues. The disease also affects areas of the brain associated with voluntary movement; these effects occur more often in men than in women. Due to the muscle rigidity, warm water is often preferred (in the mid-80s Fahrenheit, or roughly 30 degrees Celsius).

Parkinson's disease often involves challenges with balance and posture. Specifically, the posture may be stooped, with a forward head position that can precipitate a forward fall or slip if balance is compromised. Therefore, you should always use the handrails when entering or exiting the pool. Exercises should be done in the shallow end for added stability. Focusing on exercises for posture, such as the chest and back opener in (4.15), the chest press (5.26), and the horizontal shoulder abduction and adduction (5.28) will help strengthen the muscles of the upper torso which will aid in proper posture.

MUSCULAR DYSTROPHY

Muscular dystrophy is a group of inherited diseases involving the degeneration of muscles. Muscle tissue wastes away and is gradually replaced with fat and connective tissue. The disease also involves the heart and in some cases mental impairment.

Research shows that individuals with muscular dystrophy can benefit from moderate strength training or resistance training in the water in combination with stretching. Many people believe that exercise increases the degeneration of the muscles, but this effect is not demonstrated in research studies. In fact, many participants in a structured exercise plan experience greater ease in activities of daily life. An appropriate aquatic exercise program focuses on moves that target strengthening of a particular muscle or group of muscles, as well as related stretches. The exercises that focus on leg strength such as the squat (4.6), side squats (5.20) and walking lunges (5.21) will be extremely beneficial to maintaining as much muscle, and therefore strength, as possible in the lower extremities.

FIBROMYALGIA

Fibromyalgia also involves the muscles, and it affects mostly women (of all ages). It is often difficult to diagnose and is associated with widespread muscle aches, tenderness in connective tissue, and joint stiffness. The condition is believed to involve a genetic disorder in specific neurotransmitters that affect how the central nervous system processes pain. It often affects sleep and the nervous system and may be accompanied by other chronic diseases.

Persons with fibromyalgia have been shown to possess less-than-average coordination, muscular strength, and cardiovascular endurance. However, studies have also found improvement in pain symptoms and overall fitness in patients who perform cardiovascular exercise three times per week. Specifically, patients who do not exercise tend to experience compromised blood flow, which causes a buildup of acid metabolites that contribute to increased pain. On the other hand, patients who do exercise have more effective blood flow to remove the metabolites.

It is imperative to start these workouts at low intensity in order to avoid overexertion and to monitor for any increase in pain or other symptoms. Tolerances vary, but most patients are more comfortable in warm-water pools with temperatures above the mid-80s Fahrenheit (above about 30 degrees Celsius). Because symptoms tend to be worse in the morning, exercise may be more comfortable in the later afternoon or evening.

The exercise program should exclude higher-impact rebounding moves and include low-impact moves or nonimpact moves in deep water. Therefore, the exercises presented include flotation, suspended, neutral, and anchored or grounded moves. Exercise should focus on efficient muscle function, stretching to increase flexibility, and increasing mobility. Remember to listen to your body and not overexert yourself.

RHEUMATOID ARTHRITIS

Rheumatoid arthritis (RA) differs from osteoarthritis in that it affects not one isolated joint but the entire body. RA is a chronic autoimmune inflammatory disease—possibly genetic—that usually affects the smaller joints in the extremities of the hands and feet. It is more common among women than men, and onset usually occurs after the age of 40.

No one knows what causes RA. It affects the lining of the joints, which causes painful swelling that is usually worse in the morning. For this reason, you may want to schedule your aquatic exercise period for the afternoon. The swelling eventually causes bone erosion which can lead to joint deformity.

Rheumatoid arthritis tends to appear in flare-ups or periods of worsening severity that come and go. As a result, some days of exercise may be easier than others. Always listen to your body. On days when RA seems to be more uncomfortable, you may choose to omit holding on to any equipment that increases blood flow to the hands and fingers. If you want to hold a piece of equipment for added surface area or balance, choose to use the noodle instead of hand buoys. The handles on the hand buoys are smaller in diameter than the noodle, so your fingers are required to bend at a greater joint angle than if you had your hand around a noodle.

Gentle aquatic exercise can help individuals with RA by strengthening the muscles around the smaller joints and decreasing the level of fatigue. When you strengthen the muscles around the smaller joints, these muscles can function for longer periods of time without becoming fatigued. The exercises include less strenuous moves that are anchored and moves that use a flotation device to help support the body. Always check with your health care provider before you start a new exercise program—and again, always listen to your body.

EXERCISES FOR SPECIAL POPULATIONS

Remember that these exercises should be performed after a gentle warm-up of water walking and followed by a flexibility session that allows your muscles to return to their original length.

Table 16.1   Exercises for Special Populations

Exercise	Sets and reps or duration	Modification
4.1 Knee flexion and extension (p. 39)	2 sets of 12 with each leg	—
4.2 Hip flexion (p. 40)	2 sets of 12 with each leg	—
4.3 Hip extension (p. 41)	2 sets of 12 with each leg	—
4.4 Leg swing (p. 42)	2 sets of 12 with each leg	—
4.5 Calf raise (p. 43)	2 sets of 12	—

Exercise	Sets and reps or duration	Modification
4.6 Squat (p. 44)	2 sets of 12	—
4.7 Hip abduction and adduction (p. 45)	2 sets of 12 with each leg	—
4.11 Trunk rotation (p. 52)	2 sets of 12	—
4.12 Triceps push-down (p. 54)	2 sets of 12	—
4.13 Biceps curl (p. 55)	2 sets of 12	—

(continued)

Table 16.1 Exercises for Special Populations *(continued)*

Exercise	Sets and reps or duration	Modification
4.15 Chest and back opener (p. 57)	2 sets of 12	—
5.13 Neutral jack (p. 77)	2 sets of 30 seconds	Can be done while holding on to a noodle.
5.14 Neutral cross-country (p. 78)	2 sets of 30 seconds	Can be done with legs straddling a noodle.
5.18 Anchored jab punch (p. 83)	2 sets of 30 seconds	Can be done with back against wall for stability.
5.19 Anchored arm chaos (p. 84)	2 sets of 30 seconds	Can be done with back against wall for stability.

Exercise	Sets and reps or duration	Modification
5.20 Side squat (p. 85)	2 sets of 30 seconds	Can be done while holding on to wall for balance.
5.21 Walking lunge (p. 86)	2 sets of 30 seconds	Can be done while holding on to wall for balance.
5.22 Straight-leg zombie walk (p. 87)	2 sets of 30 seconds	Can be done while holding on to wall for balance.
5.23 Tightrope traveling (p. 88)	2 sets of 30 seconds	Can be done while holding on to wall for balance.
5.24 Lateral trunk flexion (p. 89)	2 sets of 12	Can be done while holding on to wall for balance.

(continued)

Table 16.1 Exercises for Special Populations *(continued)*

Exercise	Sets and reps or duration	Modification
5.26 Chest press (p. 91)	2 sets of 12	Can be done with back against wall for stability.
5.27 Straight-arm push-down (p. 92)	2 sets of 12	—
5.28 Horizontal shoulder abduction and adduction (p. 93)	2 sets of 12 with each arm	Can be done while holding on to wall for balance.
5.29 Wall push-up (p. 94)	2 sets of 12	—
5.30 Prone hip abduction and adduction (p. 95)	2 sets of 12	—

Exercise	Sets and reps or duration	Modification
6.10 Side shoot-through (p. 107)	2 sets of 30 seconds	This exercise is strictly for patients with fibromyalgia and those women who are pregnant. A growing pregnancy will cause the knees to flare out (one knee to each side) as the baby grows.
6.12 Flotation extension and abduction-adduction (p. 110)	2 sets of 30 seconds	This exercise is strictly for patients with fibromyalgia and women who are pregnant. A growing pregnancy will cause the knees to flare out (one knee to each side) as the baby grows.
6.13 Noodle balance (p. 112)	2 sets of 30 seconds	Can be done while holding on to wall for balance.
6.14 Stationary plank (p. 113)	2 sets of 30 seconds	—
6.17 Side-balance lean (p. 116)	2 sets of 30 seconds with each leg	Can be done while holding on to wall for balance.

(continued)

Table 16.1 Exercises for Special Populations *(continued)*

Exercise		Sets and reps or duration	Modification
6.18 Triceps push-up (p. 117)		2 sets of 12	—

BIBLIOGRAPHY

Abrahams, Peter (Ed.). (2007). *How the body works: A comprehensive illustrated encyclopedia of anatomy.* New York: Metro Books.

Aquatic Exercise Association. (2006). *Aquatic fitness professional manual.* Nokomis, FL: Author

Brewer, Sarah. (2009). *The human body: A visual guide to human anatomy.* New York: Metro Books.

Calais-Germain, Blandine. (1991). *Anatomy of movement.* Seattle: Eastland Press,.

Hall, Susan. (2003). Basic Biomechanics. Boston: McGraw Hill.

Hamill, Joseph, and Knutzen, Kathleen. (2003). *Biomechanical basis of human movement.* Philadelphia: Lippincott Williams & Wilkins.

Howley, Edward. and Franks, Don. (2007). *Fitness professional's handbook.* Champaign, IL: Human Kinetics.

Krumhardt, Barbara, and Alcamo, Edward. (2010). *E-Z anatomy and physiology.* Hauppauge, NY: Barron.

Luttgens, Kathyrn, and Hamilton, Nancy. (1997). *Kinesiology: Scientific basis of human movement.* Madison: Brown & Benchmark.

National Geographic. (2007). *Body: The complete human.* Washington, DC: National Geographic Society.

White, Martha. (1995). *Water exercise.* Champaign, IL: Human Kinetics.

YMCA of the USA. (2000). *YMCA water fitness for health.* Champaign, IL: Human Kinetics.

INDEX

NOTE: Page numbers followed by an italicized *t* or *f* indicate that a table, or figure, respectively, will be found on that page.

ABOUT THE AUTHOR

Melissa Layne holds a master's degree in exercise physiology from Auburn University, a bachelor's degree in physical education from Athens State University, a Georgia state teaching certificate, and fitness certifications through the Aquatic Exercise Association, the Aerobics and Fitness Association of America, and the American Council on Exercise. She has been a fitness director for several health clubs, head cheerleading coach, and an Americans with Disabilities Act specialist working with businesses to verify disability programs.

Layne is on the faculty at the University of North Georgia in the physical education department. She presents at multiple industry conferences each year, where many of her sessions feature aquatic workouts. She teaches a dozen group exercise classes per week, including aqua classes. She has starred in two SCW Fitness Education DVDs and 12 *Water in Motion* instructional exercise DVDs.